This book is dedicated to the young men who played for FC Shoreline International, and their families, as well as all kids around the world whose challenging circumstances prevent them from playing the "beautiful game".

We All Wore BLUE

EMERSON ROBBINS

ISBN 978-1-54398-044-8 (print)
ISBN 978-1-54398-045-5 (eBook)

CONTENTS

CHAPTER 1

THE KICK-OFF

I never would have imagined I'd someday be coaching a soccer team. Even though I always loved sports, I didn't know the first thing about soccer growing up, other than it was popular around the world and it was played with one's feet. They didn't have soccer where I grew up. Or if they did, I sure didn't know anything about it.

I was never a great athlete myself. I was the guy that the coach would spot playing in the gym and say, "Hey, Robbins, looking good. You should come out for the team this year." Then I'd come to tryouts and for two straight years, I was the last guy cut. No hard feelings. I deserved to be cut. I was the kid who was not quite good enough to make the team, but usually one of the best in the regular gym classes. It never stopped me from playing hoops after school in my driveway and later on in adult leagues and at the local health club.

However, when I became a father, it was pretty clear that my first-born son, Ben, was a natural athlete. When he was only about two and a half, he could throw a whiffle ball up and hit it in the air with a bat. I could see he was no chip off the ol' block. Instead, it looked like he'd own the block. I couldn't wait until he was old enough to play a sport.

My name is Emerson Robbins, known to all my friends as Skip. My brother Steve and I owned a chain of engagement ring stores, which is how I found myself one evening at a boring industry dinner dance, the kind where everyone sits around round tables and is served the proverbial chicken or fish dinner, ordered in advance. Though I always hated these types of events, it was expected for me to be there, and I'm usually a get-along kind of guy.

I was sitting at a table next to a friend of mine in the biz, Bob Sears. Bob was a sales rep for a big jewelry wholesaler. We didn't do much business together, but he and I always got along well.

His wife, Renee, was entertaining Sherri, my wife, with a story about the time, many years ago, when she went out on a date with Elvis. Yes, The Elvis!

Bob said, "Logan, my six-year-old, is having a blast playing soccer."

"Where does he play?"

"He plays through AYSO, at the Sherman Oaks Park, you know, the fields off Woodman."

AYSO is the American Youth Soccer Organization, the largest organization in the country for youth soccer, founded in Torrance, California, in 1964.

I didn't hear much about soccer growing up, as mentioned, it just wasn't played in my neck of the woods. "I've been wanting to sign Ben up for a sport. When are sign-ups?"

Bob, taking a bite from his cheesecake. "I think they're next month."

I was also thrilled that Sherri was enjoying her conversation with Renee, which hopefully meant I wouldn't have to dance.

*   *   *

So, with Bob's encouragement, I decided to sign Ben up. When the AYSO sign-ups opened, I was there first thing to register my son to play at AYSO Region 58 in Sherman Oaks.

Ben ended up on a team coached by a gentleman who looked more like a bird watcher than a coach...turned out, his hobby really was bird watching.

He even wore the dorky shorts and vest. This not-very-athletic-looking gent knew less about soccer than even I did, and, worse, he proved to be totally inept dealing with young kids, even his own.

The first season was a long one for this unfortunate team. For me, too...the boys lost every game. They didn't keep score at that age, but the kids knew what was happening. No one likes losing, especially every game. The kids learned very little about soccer, and most didn't even have fun.

On the positive side, Ben enjoyed playing and, as suspected, he turned out to be the best player on the team. Soccer at that time wasn't a very popular sport in the USA, at least not in our area. There were not many parents who understood the game or who were willing to put in the time to coach, so the league board members were always begging for volunteers.

I began to realize it was only fair to cut the bird watcher some slack... at least he was trying to make a difference, and so I decided to volunteer to coach a team. The region's directors were thrilled to have another sucker step up.

Having a somewhat obsessive personality, I spent many evenings studying the "beautiful game." I ordered books and read them cover to cover. Most of the coaches in the league came from other countries, such as Mexico, England, Scotland, Ireland, Portugal, South Africa, and other countries where the game of futbol is King and just about every boy grows up with a ball in his crib. I soon discovered that the top coach in the league was an Israeli gentleman named Abe.

I introduced myself to Abe. "They asked me to coach, but I'm fairly new to soccer, so I'm hoping I can ask you some questions every now and then. They tell me you're the man to talk to."

Abe smiled. "Sure, Skip, call me anytime." He gave me his phone number.

I took Abe up on his kind offer and called him several times a week, each time bombarding him with questions. Abe always graciously complied. I can't recall how many times I called Abe up, but I know it was quite a few and he really helped me to learn the basics.

While I didn't know much about soccer; I'd like to believe I'm a natural coach.

My first coaching gig was when I was in high school. My younger brother, Steve, then in middle school, was on a local YMCA team. Steve's Y team played baseball, basketball, flag football, track and field, even competed in swimming—just about every sport but soccer. Steve's team wasn't doing well, and one day he came home from practice and said his coach had quit, leaving the team high and dry.

No parent stepped up, so Steve asked if I'd take over as coach.

I readily agreed and ended up doing well. My very first move was to encourage Steve to recruit all the best athletes at his middle school. Being a popular kid and a great salesman, Steve ended up convincing many of the top athletes at his school to join the team. The Condors soon soared from last place to the top team in their league in just about every sport, quite a dramatic turn-around.

After the games, I'd pile Steve and his teammates into my old Chevy Nova and treat them all to ice cream. It just so happened I worked at a local Baskin-Robbins and got a discount. This was the start of my coaching career. Two seasons later, Steve graduated middle school and my coaching gig was over. I wouldn't coach again until many years later, six years after Ben was born— a 14-year hiatus from coaching.

I was born in Seattle. Though our parents moved, many of my family remained in Seattle—my grandparents, an aunt, uncle, and cousins—and so I visited the "Emerald City" often while growing up. That was how I became a die-hard Seahawks fan, starting back when the team first joined the NFL in 1976.

When I started coaching Ben's team, I knew I wasn't going to make naming the team a democratic process. I didn't want to be stuck with a team named the "Scooby Doo's," or the "Foot-Fighters," the "A-Team," or the like.

I decided to name the team The Seahawks after the team I'd rooted for ever since the franchise began.

CHAPTER 2

THE SEAHAWKS OF SOCCER

In our first season, we finished somewhere in the middle of the pack, which I thought was a fairly worthy accomplishment given I was a total neophyte to the game. The kids seemed to have a lot of fun, and the parents were complimentary about their new and enthusiastic coach. Maybe they were just cutting me some slack, knowing I was new to this. In our second season, we finished near the top of the league. There was a yearly draft in the league in order to keep parity, so the team's roster changed annually. I tried to draft the boys I wanted back, but that wasn't always possible. There were always some returning players, as well as a bunch of new players.

A key part of my success as a coach was that I had a way of making the game and practices fun for the boys, though I'd still be working them hard. I'd often bring toys as incentives, going to the Dollar Store every week to stock up. I also gave many of the boys nicknames. A short, stout defender, named Paul was "Paul the Wall" because I told him he was like a wall that no one could get past. Then there was Bobby "The Bullet," faster than a speeding bullet, and "Super Glue Glen" because he marked players so tight. Another boy was "The Hitman" because he was so tough. Jake "the Snake" was our quick moving Goal Keeper.

Back then, in the 80's, attitudes weren't nearly as politically correct as they are today, so I could get away with some of these now controversial monikers. The boys on the team seemed to take great pride in their nicknames. I innately understood how to make the game fun for the kids, which was half the battle.

By the third season, the Seahawks contended for the league championship. However, we lost the game in a tight penalty kick shoot-out. Nonetheless, this same season, we beat Abe's team, and Ben had become one of the top players in the league—obviously a huge boost to our team's success.

Another factor to my quick rise up the coaching ladder was that I knew what I didn't know and had no ego about bringing in help. Early on, I found a former college player and paid him to help train the boys at practices. I always sought out help from former players who'd played the game at a fairly high level.

When Ben was 11, I hit pay dirt. One of the office ladies who worked for my company was dating Martin Vasquez, who a few years earlier played for the U.S. National Men's Soccer Team. He'd also played professional soccer in Mexico and was still playing in the top league in the U.S. at that time.

I asked the young lady, "You think Martin might be interested in helping train my son's soccer team and earn some money on the side?"

"I'll ask him," she said, and returned a few days later. "Hey, good news! Martin is up for it."

He was soon training the boys two practices a week. Martin was planning to give his girlfriend, Denise, an engagement ring, so we worked out a deal. Instead of cash, Martin got a beautiful diamond engagement ring for training the team.

The boys were mesmerized watching Martin juggle a soccer ball, seemingly keeping it in the air forever. They benefitted greatly from having a high-caliber trainer like Martin, but they weren't the only ones.

I was like a sponge, asking Martin a thousand questions and soaking up all the knowledge I could about the world's most popular game. Before long, I found I had a pretty decent grasp of the game.

After his playing career ended, Martin went on to serve as assistant coach for the L.A. Galaxy and later for Chivas USA, also of the MLS. Then, the legendary player and coach Jurgen Klinsmann hired Martin to be his assistant coach at Bayern Munich, one of the world's top teams. He later returned to Chivas USA as head coach. He then joined Klinsmann again, this time as assistant coach for the United States Men's national team. The boys were pretty darn lucky to have such incredible training. Martin and I became friends, and Sherri and I attended Martin and Denise's wedding not long after the season ended. We still remain friends to this day.

Before the start of the fourth season, Abe suggested we team up, though I'd guess it was not because he thought I was the better Coach. More likely, it was because he thought we'd make a good combo with him training and coaching combined with my previous success, my abundant enthusiasm, and the fact that the boys on my team always seemed to have a lot of fun. Also, since Ben and Abe's sons were two of the top players in the league, Abe likely felt this union would be an advantage. Abe also figured out that I was a good evaluator of talent. When the drafts were held, I always seemed to come up with a few lower draft choices that proved to be "diamonds in the rough."

The team did well again, but the season didn't go as smoothly for me as it had before Abe and I teamed up. I decided that I preferred to coach alone. Abe's son was a great player, but he could be hard-headed. I found it wasn't easy to coach a fellow coach's son. By this time, I was recognized as one of the best coaches in the league, and I was asked to coach the Region 58 All-Star team, which I did for the next few years.

In 1987, Ben and Abe's son, David were invited to play on a Southern California All-Star team. The team was heading overseas to play against youth teams in Japan, Malaysia, Singapore, and Hong Kong. Neither Abe nor I were coaching this team, but we still jumped at the opportunity. The team met in the West L.A. area and practiced for several months prior to the trip. One of the players' dads was an international travel agent and made all of the arrangements for the families that went. The group of boys and their parents had a great time on this trip, combining the many games with lots of sightseeing. Ben turned out to be one of the top players, even on this team made up of All-Stars from all over Southern California.

Ben was only about four years old when his mother and I divorced. We'd been high school sweethearts in our senior year, but it wasn't long into our marriage that we realized we'd made a big mistake. We were polar opposites in many ways, coming from completely different backgrounds and having very little in common; we had no business getting married. Nevertheless, we stuck it out for seven years and had two children—Ben, our firstborn, and Kerri, his younger sister, who was barely a year old at the time of our separation. Not long after we separated, I met Sherri and fell in love. Sherri was and is a vivacious blonde, about 5'2" with a warm smile, a magnetic personality, and a heart of gold. We dated for several years after the divorce. After the traumatic ending of my first marriage, I was naturally "gun-shy." I was the first in my family to get a divorce. My parents had a marriage made in heaven, so I came from a happy home and wanted no less for myself and my children. Everyone who met Sherri loved her, though none more than me. The two of us seemed to belong together and, as time would prove, we most certainly did.

Ben, as well as my daughter, Kerri, took to Sherri, and she became like a best friend, never trying or wanting to be their second mother. Ben was 11 when Sherri and I tied the knot, with Ben serving as my handsome best man and Kerri as our adorable auburn-haired flower girl.

It was now 1989. Ben had turned 12 and was entering middle school. He'd been playing soccer since he was six years old. He also played basketball for almost as long. Ben loved both games and excelled at both, but since the two sports took place in the same season, he was forced to make a choice when he began middle school. Soccer or basketball? This was a really tough decision. Although I loved coaching soccer, I knew it was my job as a dad to advise Ben to follow his heart. After much thought and deliberation, he finally decided on basketball over soccer. This was not what I'd hoped for, but it was Ben's decision to make. All I could do was gulp and fully embrace his decision. I was then retired from coaching soccer, at least for a while.

A year earlier, in 1988, Sherri and I had our first child, Ryan, and when Ryan was five, I eagerly signed him up for soccer. Ryan was not the athlete that Ben was, but that didn't matter. I just wanted him to have fun, get some exercise and as an added bonus, I was back coaching again.

However, I soon found out that coaching five-year-old boys is more like babysitting than coaching. Nevertheless, I stayed with it for Ryan's sake. By the time Ryan was around seven, I found it again enjoyable to coach. I made sure to keep it fun for Ryan and the other boys on the team, and we did well. The Seahawks were back, contending for the league championship just about every season.

Ryan had a completely different nature than Ben and as parents often do, if they're open to it, I learned some valuable lessons from my kids. Ben was intense, driven to be the best he could be, while Ryan was a politician, more of a peacemaker. There was a boy in Ryan's kindergarten class, Jonathon, nicknamed Jono, who was the proverbial class bully. Having heard from Ryan several times that Jono was picking on him and some of the other kids, Ben and I advised him, that in order to get it to stop, all Ryan needed to do was to punch him in the nose one time. That way, we told Ryan, he'd never be bullied again, at least not by Jono. So, we proceeded to teach Ryan how to throw a punch, shadow boxing with him the next few afternoons. A few days later, at dinner, we asked Ryan if he had punched Jono yet? Ryan responded, no; instead, he'd decided to make friends with Jono, which he did. This was Ryan personified. A wise five-year-old had clearly taught us a better way to handle things.

As it turned it out, Jono and Ryan became good friends. As luck would have it, or maybe karma playing its part, Jono happened to develop into one of the best soccer players in the league and because he and Ryan were friends, I later drafted him on our team. With Jono's athleticism and soccer skills playing a key part, the Seahawks were back, contending for the league championship just about every season thereafter.

Three years after Ryan was born, Sherri and I had another son, Tyler, and when Tyler was five, I signed him up for soccer as well. Since I didn't have the time to coach two teams and I sure didn't want to start all over again with preschoolers, I didn't coach Tyler's team the first year. I served as an assistant coach for Tyler's team the following year, while I continued to coach the Seahawks—now the perennial league leaders. I was now among the most respected coaches in the league, and several other coaches were asking for my advice, just as I had with Abe many years prior.

Meanwhile, Ben was now a varsity starter, two-time captain of his high school basketball team, and one of the best players in his league. His high school team became one of the top teams in Southern California when, in Ben's junior year, his school welcomed the Twin Towers, the Collins twins, Jason and Jarron, each almost seven feet tall. These twins, both bright and extremely nice young men, were dominating inside players, while Ben served as the captain and point guard, feeding the twins the ball and hitting three pointers when the defense collapsed. Ben set a new school record for assists, as well as three pointers. The Collins twins later went on to play for Stanford University and from there, to the NBA.

I loved watching Ben play. In the four years that Ben played for his Harvard-Westlake High School team, I didn't miss a game, not even an away game. I was not, however, very fond of his coach. The coach often wore a cheesy lime green suit with cowboy boots, obviously a real fashion hound. Bear in mind, he dressed like this in L.A. at one of the top prep schools in the state. This humorless jerk was careful never to shout at the twins, but he'd often get in the face of some of the other players and scream at them at the top of his voice, humiliating them in the echoing gym in front of all their friends, folks, and fans.

More often than not, I regret it if I tell someone off. However, in this case, I look back and regret not telling Ben's coach what I thought of him. I would never have done so when Ben was playing for him, but wished I had after he graduated. What also was disturbing, was that although Ben was the captain and the star guard for his team for several years, this tacky and tactless coach never went even one step out of his way to help Ben in his quest to play basketball in college.

Ben ended up playing a few years of college ball, but no thanks to his high school coach. The only saving grace of this coach was by watching him interact with his players, he unintentionally taught me what *not* to do as a coach.

I was juggling going to Ben's basketball games and helping coach two youth soccer teams, all while running a business. Fortunately, I was partners with my brother Steve in our now very successful chain of engagement ring stores, so I somehow managed to take time off to go to Ben's games and still coach my other two boys.

I ran the creative side of the business, the marketing, merchandising, and store design, while Steve handled daily store operations as well as the finances. We were close, and each of us proved to be experts in our given areas. I had great respect for Steve's financial acumen and his sales ability. However, as anyone who's ever been in a family business knows, it's often difficult to mix family and business. Steve was ambitious and the main driver of the business, while I wasn't nearly as driven and wanted more balance in my life. I was making more money than I'd ever dreamed of, but I was growing tired of feeling like second fiddle. We were both type A personalities, and it's never easy to have two drivers for one car.

In spite of the money I was making, I was no longer enjoying the business, feeling more and more like a partner in title only and finding myself becoming increasingly cynical and bitter. I loved my younger brother and had tremendous respect for him. I had no illusions about who was the better businessman, and I knew that if I went my own way, it was not likely that I'd earn as much as I was making at that time. However, I'd also learned a valuable lesson— money doesn't make you happy. I wished things could be different, but after so many years working together; I finally accepted the fact that Steve wasn't going to change. So, after many years of frustration, I finally decided to sell him my share of the business.

More than anything else, I wanted to continue loving my brother, but I had come to the conclusion this couldn't be sustained unless I moved on—an extremely difficult and emotional decision that I'd pondered for several years. It was now the right time to move on. Both of my older children from my first marriage, Ben and Kerri, had graduated high school and were either already in or were headed off to college. Sherri and I spent a great deal of time discussing this, and finally decided it was the perfect time in our lives to leave Southern California.

At the season's end, as was the norm for all teams, the Seahawks held the team banquet after our final season as a team. Sherri and I had grown close to many of the players and parents. While the team roster would change every year, a handful of players had remained on the team for several years, a few even since the team's inception.

Most of them had heard and were disappointed to find out I was moving to Seattle. One of the players, a talented little guy named Andy, had a dad who was the noted sportscaster, Roy Firestone. Andy was one of the stars of the team, which had just come off a great year, vying once again for the league title. Roy, known to just about every sports fan in Southern California and beyond, gave a heartfelt speech about what a great coach I was for the kids and how much his son loved the team and this season—his son's favorite season ever. This was already an emotional day for me, and being an emotional guy to begin with, I could barely keep it together. With tears in my eyes, I choked out a warm and genuine thank you to Roy and all of the players, parents, and friends who attended the event. The team handed me a goodbye gift, suitably an umbrella, knowing our family was headed up to the rainy Northwest.

CHAPTER 3

THE MOVE TO SEATTLE

As mentioned, being born in Seattle and having visited there just about every year of my life, I always had an affinity for the Northwest and somehow knew I'd return there someday. Sherri had spent several summers in the Northwest, visiting her aunt and uncle, who had a vacation home on Orcas Island in the San Juans, so she also had fond memories of her visits.

So, in 1998, when Ryan was about 10 years old and Tyler seven, we packed up our old Volvo 240 station wagon and took a drive up the Pacific Coast. Sherri and I knew we wanted to live near the coast, but we weren't sure exactly where. After stopping off and checking out a number of small towns and cities along the coast, we finally decided we felt most at home in the Seattle area. After looking at dozens of houses, we ended up buying a cool mid-century home on a bluff with expansive views of Puget Sound, in Shoreline, Washington, just north of Seattle.

When soccer season rolled around, Ryan got on a team that had played together for many years and had been coached throughout by the same gentleman. There was no opportunity for me to coach this team. Tyler also got on a team that already had a coach or, as it turned out, co-coaches. It didn't matter much to me, as I had my hands more than full starting a new business in a new city. I went to watch my boys play and often had to bite my lip, feeling I could do a better job of coaching.

Tyler's team was especially tough to watch. They were truly the Bad News Bears of soccer. Named the Thunder-Foots, they hadn't won a single game since their inception, three seasons earlier.

After a few weeks, I got to know Carol, one of the players' moms, and we often chatted while watching the games. Carol's son, Connor, was one of the team's better players. Carol was frustrated watching the team play, but being a dignified and professional woman, tried to stay positive. Being a psychologist, this wasn't overly difficult for her. At the same time, I didn't have what one would call a poker-face, so it didn't take any psycho-analysis for Carol to notice my frustration.

She learned that I'd coached soccer in Southern California and felt that the two dads who had been coaching the team for years really didn't want to coach but were doing so because no one else had stepped up when the team was first formed three seasons earlier. Being a former athlete, Carol had thought about coaching herself, but she had a busy family psychology practice and was unable to make the two practices each week.

I was hesitant to step on anyone's toes, especially since my son was a recent addition to the team when, on her own, Carol decided to see if the coaches had any interest in seeking my help. She first spoke with George, one of the co-coaches. He confessed that he'd love to step down, freely admitting that he wasn't any kind of expert of the game and would much prefer to just be a dad and watch his son Patrick play. Carol then spoke with Bill, the other co-coach. Bill looked like the guy who'd been the star quarterback in high school. He also jumped at the opportunity to step back and turn the team over to me.

He ran a local chain of supermarkets and felt he'd been devoting too much time to coaching.

He too just wanted to watch his son, Sam, play and let someone who knew the game better take over. A few weeks later, when the season ended, at the Thunder-Foots team party, Carol shared the conversations she had with both of the coaches.

I replied, "If Bill and George are absolutely sure they don't want to keep coaching, I'll be glad to step in. I do miss it."

Our move up to the Northwest proved to be a great decision. I was able to start a new business and do it my way. Although I didn't have the financial security I had while partners with my brother, I could now make quick decisions without having to thrash things out with a partner, and I could build the business based on my own ideas and philosophies.

I soon built a thriving business in the industry I knew best, starting with one small engagement ring boutique in Belltown, a neighborhood in downtown Seattle.

I discovered that youth soccer in Washington was quite a bit different from how it had been in Southern California. For one thing, soccer seemed to be more popular in the Northwest. One would see youth soccer teams playing on just about every grass field around every afternoon and weekend. When I attended North Hollywood High School, the schools in the area didn't even have soccer teams, yet here in the Seattle area, I discovered that many of the men around my age had played soccer in high school. There also was no AYSO in Washington State. Instead, youth soccer, at least in our area, was through the SYSA, the Seattle Youth Soccer Association, a branch of the larger state entity, the WSYSA, the Washington State Youth Soccer Association.

There were three levels of soccer at the younger recreational ages, and an additional eight levels of club soccer for the older ages; eleven in all. The entry level, termed recreational soccer, was the level the Thunder-Foots played at.

In the primary years, leagues didn't keep standings and, given the Thunder-Foots' record over the first three years, that was a blessing, for if they had, the team would've had an ironclad hold of the cellar—the worst team in the league.

Being a marketing guy, the first thing I did upon taking over the reins was change the team's name. No more Thunder-Foots. Naming the team would, again, not be a democratic process. I imagined how the team was first named the Thunder-Foots. I knew that no adult would've chosen that name.

Like most families, we considered our dog to be part of the family. Moose was a Jack Russell with a stout, muscular body, short legs, and white fur with large and small black spots. He had a black patch over one eye, just like the dog from the *Little Rascals* or the vintage RCA dog. He was like a cartoon character; his looks always drew a smile from anyone passing by. Little did they know that Moose was a fearless hunter of squirrels, possums, rats, mice, raccoons, and other furry little creatures. Moose thus inspired our team's new name—the Mad Dogs.

The Mad Dogs were now a new team, with a new coach, but with most of the same players. The team looked like the typical suburban, white, middle-class group of boys you'd find playing youth soccer in just about any area of the country.

There was no draft system in Washington like they had in the AYSO in Southern California, so players stayed on the same team for several years unless they requested a change.

The team had a few decent players, including Bill's son (Bill, the former co-coach), Sam, Carol's son Connor, the other co-coach's son, Patrick, and the new assistant coach, Mark's son, Max, as well as a few others who showed some promise. Once we began practicing, I was surprised the team hadn't won at least a few games over the past years.

That first season I took over, the boys only nine years old, the league still didn't keep official standings, but the team finally won enough games to finish in the middle of the pack. The highlight of the season was when our newly organized Mad Dogs pulled off a huge upset, beating the dreaded Blue Knights, the top team in the league—a team that hadn't lost a game in three years—still one of the greatest upsets of my coaching career.

As I had in seasons past, I continued to make playing soccer fun for the boys, while bringing a more competitive approach to the team, one returning players hadn't experienced before. I wanted them to have fun, but also knew its more fun to win than it is to lose. Practices were now a lot more organized and more serious than before I took over.

I taught the boys how to control the ball, how to play defense, how to play as a team, installed formations, the first time the boys were exposed to most of these soccer fundamentals. I continued my tradition of bringing toys to the practices and created "Mad Dog University," where the players were taught the basics in soccer both on and off the field. They studied written material and answered questions, as well as demonstrated newly taught skills on the field. There were tests on accuracy in passing, on how to defend, dribbling around cones, shooting on goal and many other skills including testing their knowledge of soccer. The boys were provided with information sheets and expected to learn assorted aspects of the game including how to properly prepare for a game, "The Principles of Defense", the names for the various parts of the field, "The Coaches Top Ten Soccer Sins", some of the basic rules of soccer and more... This information was then taught and reviewed at almost every practice.

I also shared with them a quote from the most famous soccer player of all-time, the great Pele', who said, "Success is no accident, it is the result of hard work, perseverance, learning, sacrifice and most of all, a love for what you are learning and doing."

At mid-season, the Mad Dog University finals would be held, where boys who correctly answered the most questions about soccer could pick out a toy in priority order based on how many points they'd scored. If a player didn't do well on the final, he still got to pick a toy, though later in the pecking order.

When a player didn't test well, I'd spend time bringing him up to snuff. The majority of the players and parents seemed to be thrilled that the boys were learning a lot more about soccer and showing vast improvement on the field.

A few of the lesser skilled boys didn't want to take soccer so seriously, which is why one or two didn't return the next season, or maybe it was just because as the boys grew older, only those who really loved the game kept playing.

I found coaching to be very similar to running a business, which I had great experience in and an obvious talent for. A successful business, at least from my perspective, required the owner to seek out talent. No business or team could be expected to be successful without having talent. Once you've found the talent, you then needed to provide the associates or the players with effective training. You needed to follow through with this by making sure your company or your team consistently executed the fundamentals that you had taught and trained. And you had to make sure to keep the troops motivated. I've always felt people perform better when their efforts are directly or indirectly rewarded, either financially and/or in the case of a soccer team, emotionally.

In other words, players are provided with positive reinforcement. Numerous, but always sincere compliments, pats on the back, make sure your associates or players know that you truly care about them. Find out what they are doing well and be sure to compliment them on those strengths. Find out what they need to improve on and gently and empathetically help teach them to do better. Lastly—whether employees, associates, or players—people should enjoy coming to work or to practice or to a game. We all perform better when we're having fun.

The Mad Dogs' second season was the first time that the league kept official standings. There were many teams in the league, so the teams were separated into three groups based on the team record over the past few years.

Even though the league hadn't kept official standings earlier, they kept track internally to make sure the various leagues would be as well balanced as possible.

The Mad Dogs were placed in the bottom bracket to start, the Bronze Division, likely due to the fact the former Thunder-Foots had such a dismal record.

Above this level was the Silver Division, and the highest division at the recreational level was the Gold Division. This was a fair system, similar to how it's done in professional leagues in England and elsewhere around the world. England and other countries have as many as seven or more divisions. Based on their finish each year within their division, the top several teams move up to a higher division, while the bottom teams move down to a lower division. This system, known as promotion and relegation, is the traditional manner in which leagues keep parity in the competition.

The Seattle Youth Soccer Organization ran their recreational leagues similarly, though teams could request to move up or stay in their same division, unless they had dominated the league. Only the top two teams usually moved up, and the bottom two moved down.

By 2001, my son Tyler had become good friends with a schoolmate named Peter Yoshikawa, who lived a few blocks away. Peter was from Japan and happened to be one of the best, if not the best, athletes at Tyler's school. Peter played soccer, but on a different team, and he was also a promising baseball player.

Because Peter was over at our house quite often, Tyler, with some encouraging words from me, convinced Peter to join the Mad Dogs. While this may not have been entirely kosher, the league didn't have any firm rules against players switching teams. Other players also occasionally changed teams from one season to another so they could play with their friends. Peter had also heard about the toys I gave out and the fun his other schoolmates had playing for the Mad Dogs. It wasn't too tough a sell.

Another key player, Tim Aspinall from England, joined the Mad Dogs as well. Tim's family were all huge Manchester United fans. They never missed a game, even if it meant waking up at 4:00 a.m. to watch it. Tim's older brother, Tony was on the same team with Ryan, so I got to know Tim and his family when we were all at Ryan's and Tony's team games

Tim was the top player on the Blue Knights, the team the Mad Dogs had upset the season before. While he and his dad hadn't been overjoyed losing to the lowly Mad Dogs, they were impressed with my coaching and appreciated the fact the Mad Dogs took soccer more seriously than other teams did.

I welcomed Tim to the team, and also asked his dad, Robert, to be an assistant coach. Robert gladly accepted the position.

Peter and Tim joining the Mad Dogs proved to be pivotal. With players like Peter and Tim, plus the better players left from the original team, our team easily won the Bronze Division and moved up to the more competitive Silver Division for the following season.

On picture day, the teams would all line up for their team photo. Every season, Moose, our team mascot, would be right up front. I'd ask the photographer to shout "Moose, squirrel" right before he took the picture. This insured that Moose would be looking directly at the camera and not off into the nearby woods. This became an annual tradition, and the photographer, though he'd photographed hundreds of teams around the region, came to know the Mad Dogs and always remembered how to get Moose's attention.

In 2002, the Mad Dogs were not yet "international".
The team looked like any other suburban rec team.
Team mascot, Moose after the photographer yells "Moose, squirrel"

It was 2002. Tyler and the boys on the team were now 11 years old, and the Mad Dogs were in the Silver Division.

The team roster didn't change much from the previous season. Though I always encouraged and worked just as much with the less talented players as I did with the stronger players, nevertheless, the two weakest players dropped off the team, and two more skilled players took their place. Having never been a superior athlete myself, I appreciated any player who was willing to work hard and I truly wanted everyone on the team to have fun playing the game. However, just like all of us, kids usually prefer what they feel they're good at, so it wasn't uncommon to find that the kids who weren't quite as talented, would often move on to try another sport or some other activity. Based on the fact that in rec soccer, every player was required to play half the game, when one or two of the less skilled players dropped off, it could make a significant difference. Another change, was by this age, it was time for me to dispense with giving out toys. The boys were now old enough to enjoy the game for what it was, without having to receive a toy or some other reward for their efforts and accomplishments. Just playing the game was reward enough by this age.

The Silver Division was a big step up from Bronze, and the Mad Dogs ended up finishing in 2nd place, missing out on 1st by one game. Peter became the team's starting striker and leading scorer, and Tim excelled as the center mid, both vital positions. Sam, one of the original Thunder-Foots, also developed into a talented center defender. The team was solid up the middle.

That year, because the standings were so closely bunched, the league moved up only the first-place team, so the Mad Dogs played in the Silver Division again that next season. Once again, our team lost two of the weaker players and added two skilled players in their place. Most players on the team were now fairly skilled, so there was not much of a drop-off when I subbed players in and out of the game.

By this age—12 years old—the less serious and less skilled players, for a variety of reasons, had quit playing soccer. This was true for just about every recreational soccer league. As the age level increased, the number of teams in that particular league usually decreased. Less than half the original group that played for the Thunder-Foots now remained. There was one other big change. The Mad Dogs played in an indoor soccer league during the off-season, which helped improve the boys' foot skills. However, during one indoor game we were crushed by a club team with players a year younger.

I was impressed with the passing skills of the younger team, and asked their coach how he got his players to pass so well. The coach was a big blond guy of Dutch ancestry, about 30 years old and around 6'4", 220 lbs. His name was Russ, and he was a paid coach, as most club coaches are. Russ and I soon worked out an arrangement in which he would help train our team. He lived fairly close by and worked the graveyard shift at nearby Boeing Company.

Russ helped toughen up the Mad Dogs. At times, I felt he was almost sadistic, and I definitely had some concerns about that. Russ led one training session when he'd punt the ball 40 or more yards, sending it halfway across the field and high up in the air, where the awaiting player had to head the ball the first time. If the player didn't head it the first time, he had to go again until he successfully headed the ball. I hadn't worked on heading much as I was concerned about the players' health and safety. Russ urged me to relax, saying the boys were now old enough to learn those skills. I recalled times when dusk had settled in, yet a few of the boys were still out there, trying to successfully head the ball in the near dark field.

Russ also held a drill the players nicknamed the "Fear Drill." The boys lined up one behind another, about 10 yards from Russ. He'd kick the ball straight at them, while each player ran toward him as fast as they could. If the player paused, jumped, or turned away, he had to repeat the drill. If he ran fast and didn't hesitate or jump, the hard-struck ball would hit the boy in his shin-guards, where it wouldn't hurt much. However, if the player paused, ducked, or turned, God only knew where the ball would whack him. The boys became men over the course of this season, no longer hesitating to head or run through balls and, in doing so, our team won every game we played. The boys' passing and ball control, as well as a myriad of other soccer skills, improved through the year.

I still had concerns about Russ and some of his methods. Every practice, while the boys sat in a circle and stretched, Russ would kick balls from 50 feet away and try to hit one of them. There was no purpose to this. This wasn't training; it was more like abuse.

Maybe Russ thought it was funny, but I didn't, and finally asked him to stop. He'd agree to stop doing that, then a few practices later, Russ would be right back at it.

Nevertheless, in our second season in the Silver Division, the Mad Dogs went undefeated. I couldn't argue with the results—much of the team's success was attributable to Russ.

It was 2004, and the Mad Dogs were now in the Gold Division, "the big leagues," well, at least, the recreational big league. The team had come a long way from the bottom of the barrel, climbing its way up to making the Gold Division. The Gold Division was a big jump up from Silver. More big changes lay ahead.

CHAPTER 4

MAD DOGS AND (OTHER) COUNTRYMEN

One day, while the team practiced in the park, I eyed a tall black boy sitting in the grass, attentively watching the team practice. I could tell the boy was hoping to be invited to play, so I walked over and said, "Hi, I'm Skip, the coach. What's your name?"

"Jamal," the boy said softly, his eyes darting with caution.

"Nice to meet you, Jamal," I said. "You live close by?"

"Yes, close here."

I smiled. "You play soccer?"

Jamal nodded and his eyes widened. "Yes."

"Great," I said and motioned toward the field. "How about coming over and joining our practice?"

The boy's dark eyes widened further. "Okay."

Jamal turned out to be a decent soccer player, though it was apparent he wouldn't be a star on the team. That didn't matter. Jamal had a blast practicing, and he showed up again the next practice. I offered Jamal a spot on the team and was able to ascertain that he and his family had moved to Seattle just a few weeks prior and were living in subsidized apartments, a few blocks from the park.

I felt good about inviting Jamal to join, especially given his circumstances. Jamal had never played on a real team before. He hadn't even played with a real soccer ball before. Where he grew up, kids tied rags together to jerry-rig a ball.

Jamal mentioned he had a younger brother who'd also love to play. Yaqub, barely a year younger, was invited to the next practice, and he too was offered a spot on the Mad Dogs team. Little did I know it at the time, but adding these brothers would be the beginning of a major team metamorphosis.

I relished having the brothers from Africa on the team. They were born in Ethiopia and had come to the United States after living in a refugee camp in Kenya for most of their childhood. Their family fled their native country due to wars between religious and political factions. While in the refugee camp, going to school was not an option. When it rained, the camp flooded, so malaria and dengue fever were often rampant. Their father passed away from dysentery. The horrors they encountered were unimaginable to most Americans.

The family was clearly struggling and now having gotten to know their situation better, my heart went out to them. Every so often, I'd head to the market after practice and drop off bags of groceries for the family. I also bought them an Oromo-English dictionary so that they could translate their native language into English and English into Oromo. This would help them to improve their English as well as help them do their homework. Both the brothers appreciated being in school and worked hard to learn the language and get decent grades. They'd stay up into all hours of the night doing their homework, putting in many times the effort any

American or English-speaking student had to, and they also worked as hard as anyone on the team at all of the practices.

Coming from a horrendous place and facing challenging life experiences, playing on the Mad Dogs had to be a dream come true for the two boys.

They had now made many new friends. They were given professional-style uniforms and new cleats and many other items they couldn't have envisioned owning a year ago.

I treated them to their first slice of pizza, their first hamburger, their first time at a movie theater and more... Soccer had literally transformed their lives.

Peter and Tim were the co-captains now. They loved the game and were driven to be as good as they could possibly be. Their leadership helped shape the team's work ethic. Few if any teams worked harder than the Mad Dogs, much of which was attributable to these great co- captains, leading by example.

Gold Division was the most competitive level in recreational soccer. The only level higher than this was club soccer. Club teams operated quite differently from rec teams. They were required to hold tryouts every year. There were no rules for club teams about how much time a player had to be played. It was much more competitive than rec soccer, where all of the coaches were volunteers, usually moms or dads. Most club teams hired paid coaches. Club player fees usually started at about $1,500 and averaged at least $2,000 to $4,000 per player. Some club fees ran upwards of $5,000 a year per player, factoring in tournament fees, travel costs, additional equipment, and training. Usually only players from more affluent families could afford to play club soccer.

I was content to continue coaching recreational soccer, as I was coaching for the fun of it and to help the players learn and enjoy the game.

*   *   *

The Mad Dogs were in the big leagues. Russ was still training the boys once or twice a week, and I'd coach at the games.

In 2004, the roster hadn't changed a great deal from the previous year. Our weakest player dropped off, likely due to Russ's aggressive trainings, and the team added a player from China, whose father was a visiting professor at the University of Washington. The team did fairly well, finishing somewhere in the middle of the pack, not too shabby given the move up to the Gold Division, but still the worst finish in many years for any team I'd coached.

Jamal and Yaqub, no longer rookies, were now comfortable with the other players on the team, as well as with me, and I learned more about their background.

A few years after their father had died, their mother, Amane, met and married a man named Alo while they were in the Kenyan refugee camp. Shortly after, Alo had an opportunity for a job in the U.S. at a meat-packing plant in South Dakota. If he worked there for a few years, he could sponsor Amane and her family, which included Jamal, Yaqub, two sisters, and two other brothers—seven in all—and bring them all to live in the U.S.

After working at the plant for a few years, Alo was finally eligible to sponsor the family and bring them to the United States. The family was set to leave Kenya and make the long journey to South Dakota when, while the family was in route, Alo fell down a steep stairwell while working at the meat-packing plant and suffered brain damage resulting in periodic blackouts and convulsions. Alo could no longer work. The family had no idea this had happened until they arrived in Seattle.

Amane, the mother, was extremely shy and spoke only limited English. The family was now left without any support other than government assistance. Fortunately, they were provided with emergency-status subsidized housing.

Now more aware than ever how bleak their circumstances really were, I brought over groceries more often and drove Amane to Seattle to help her navigate the bureaucracy of the complex social services. The middle school offered an ESL class (English as a second language), and Jamal and Yaqub registered in the class. Having much in common with other ESL students, the affable brothers made friends with many of the students in their class. Since soccer is the world's most popular sport and because Jamal and Yaqub were talking up the Mad Dogs, several other ESL kids wanted to join the team.

One of them was Pemba Sherpa from Nepal. Pemba's father, Lakpa Sherpa, was one of the world's top Sherpa guides. Sherpas are an ethnic group in Nepal famous as the rugged guides who lead expeditions up the world's tallest mountains. Lakpa had summited Mount Everest over a dozen times, as well as many other of the most challenging mountains in the world. Their family moved to the Northwest when Lakpa was hired by a Seattle-based mountain climbing company to lead expeditions up Mount Rainier, Mount Adams, Mount McKinley (later re-named Denali), and other mountains, both in the U.S. and around the world. Pemba, the apple not falling far from the tree, was wiry, athletic, tough, and determined, and soon became one of the Mad Dogs' best defenders, though he also had never played organized soccer before.

Around the same time Pemba joined the team, the coach of a rival team told me that his team was breaking up and wondered if I would be willing to pick up a few of their players, including his son, the assistant coach's son, and one other player.

I knew they had a few talented players on this team, but also knew the coach's son wasn't really up to the now improved Mad Dog player level. He would make a decent back-up goal keeper and the assistant coach's son was a strong player, as was the third player. Therefore, I decided that it was worth it to add the coach's son if it meant we would pick up two strong players.

The assistant coach, Gary, and his son, Aaron, were from Fiji, as was the son's friend, Shivy. Gary wanted to be an assistant coach with the Mad

Dogs. I agreed and added the three players. Gary was a very nice man, who'd played soccer his entire life, but he wasn't exactly an experienced coach. When the team was down, his "strategic" advice was to anxiously comment, "Skip, we need to score," to which I'd usually reply, "Gary, don't you think they're trying to score?"

Gary also loved to tell the same Sarah Palin joke over and over. The boys would laugh, not at the joke, but at the fact they'd heard it so many times. It was a lot of fun to have these new families on the team, and Gary and Shivy's father, Ashwin, cooked up the best curry dishes I'd ever tasted.

I found out from Ashwin that they had moved to the U.S. when Shivy was eight or nine years old. The family had a sugar cane plantation in Fiji that had been in their family for three generations, ever since their great grandfather had moved his family there from India. The plantation was trying to support several families, over 17 people in all. The house was small, and the families were living cramped in a tiny space with barely enough food for all of them, so Ashwin sought out a better life.

Plus, there had been a military coup just a few years prior, and if there was another, he felt they would be in danger of losing their property, as had happened to other families they knew of. For six straight years, he entered a lottery that determined who could emigrate to the United States.

Only 50,000 families qualified each year. For five years, no luck, until that sixth year, they finally won the lottery! Ashwin and his wife, Camry, and their family could now legally come to the U.S. They had to spend their entire life savings on airfare to bring their family to the U.S. They had a cousin in Vancouver, British Columbia, who told them he had a friend in Washington, who would let them stay with him and would help him find a job. The only Washington that Ashwin knew of was Washington, D.C., and so that's where he thought the family was headed. However, they landed in Seattle where Ashwin learned that they were in the State of Washington and not the nation's capital, as he'd previously thought.

They found their way to the cousin's friend's apartment and stayed there until Ashwin was able to find a job three weeks later. He landed a job in accounts payable at a big company located on the 6th floor of a downtown building. Back in Fiji, Ashwin and the family had never even seen a building taller than two stories. He was employed there for a few years until the company downsized. This was in 2001, when the Twin Towers came crashing down. After this, Ashwin found it difficult to land another job. He wasn't even able to secure interviews, until he figured out that his foreign sounding name was preventing companies from wanting to hire him. So, he decided to change his first name on his resume to Eric. This change immediately paid off, as he not only got interviews with his Americanized first name, but he soon found an even better job than he'd had before.

Shivy would soon prove to be a great outside mid. He was one of the fastest on the team, and he could dribble at top speed, with the skills and ball control to elude defenders and get to the goal line where he would often send beautiful crosses into the box, that his teammates could easily knock into the goal. And Shivy also could turn to goal and score himself with a well-targeted shot.

One more highly influential change was in the works. I heard from Jamal and Aaron about another ESL student from Gambia, Essa, who already had a reputation as being a talented soccer player as well as the star running back on the middle school football team. Rumor had it he was super-fast and had slick moves. I encouraged Jamal and Aaron to invite Essa to practice. Essa showed up a few days later, and it didn't take but a few minutes to see that Essa could be a game changer for the team. Essa loved soccer and was thrilled to join the Mad Dogs.

Essa and his family moved from Gambia to the U.S. when Essa was 10 years old. Gambia was originally colonized by England, so English was taught in the schools, therefore there was no language barrier with Essa. The family moved to find more opportunity. Though Gambia was a relatively peaceful country, they had seen the military government seize some of their friends' and family members' houses and possessions. The family was fearful of this happening to them as well. At that time, Gambia was controlled by Yahya Jammeh, the strong-armed military leader who'd taken control of the country from 2006 to 2017.

Essa's father, Sainey, had been a veterinarian in his native country, but had to work in a 7-Eleven after moving to the U.S. Essa's mother, Amie, was a teacher at the local elementary school in their Gambian neighborhood prior to moving. She found work, helping out in senior retirement homes after moving to the U.S. Amie became one of the favorite moms on the team, always welcoming the boys to their home. Amie was a bundle of love and happiest when their modest rental house was filled with the mayhem of boys, either all sleeping over, or her cooking them her Gambian Yassa chicken or fried rice with lamb or goat.

With all of these new players from other countries, the Mad Dogs were a drastically different team than they'd been in their Thunder-Foot days. They now had more players from other countries than they did American-born players, and the team was now the best it had ever been.

That summer, 2004, Sherri and I took the team down to Anaheim, California, to play in a tournament for rec teams. There weren't many rec tournaments in Washington, but the main purpose for the trip was to bond as a team and just have fun. The fields for the tournament were only a few miles from Disneyland. I couldn't wait to take the guys to Disneyland, as most of them had never seen anything remotely like "the happiest place on earth" as Disneyland is often called.

A few of the players whose parents could afford to pay their son's way did so, some helped as much as they could, paying a portion of the cost, but most of the families couldn't afford to pay anything. Sherri and I were honored to pay for the flights, the hotel rooms, meals, and Disneyland tickets. We used all of the airline miles we'd earned on our credit cards the past few years to help for the boys' flights and then started building up the mileage again by paying all of the other trip expenses for the team.

Russ heard about the trip and asked to come along as well. Needing another chaperone for the boys, I told him I'd pay his way, but also made it clear, if he came and I paid his way, he'd have to share the responsibility of looking after the boys. Russ then asked if he could bring along his girlfriend, explaining that he'd pay her airfare and because I was already paying for his hotel room, it wouldn't cost me anymore. I agreed, but again reemphasized that I was paying his way, so that he would help Sherri and I keep a watchful eye on the boys.

I rented one van, but couldn't find another van to rent or any vehicle large enough to accommodate all the boys, 18 in all. So, I finally had to resort to ordering a stretch Hummer limousine. That was the only way, along with the van, we would be able to bring all the players to and from the games. Although the limo definitely cost more than it did to rent another van, it was still quite a bit less than it would have been to charter a bus.

I imagine the other teams must have been impressed or at least curious seeing the Mad Dogs pull up to the tournament in a stretch limo. Naturally, the boys fought over who would get to ride in the limo. The only fair way was they had to take turns.

Being a fairly small tournament, we only played a few games, all of which the team won handily. This trip was more about the guys having fun than it was about playing soccer, so it was off to Disneyland where the boys went on just about every ride in the park.

Russ's girlfriend turned out to be a nightmare. A compulsive talker and a nervous wreck, Russ and she would often disappear, Russ neglecting his responsibility to help watch the boys. Whenever the team had a meal together, the boys would do everything they could to avoid sitting near Russ's girlfriend. Russ was becoming more and more of a problem as time went on. Fortunately, no one got lost and the team returned to Seattle safely and without suffering any major catastrophes on the trip.

*   *   *

It was 2005, and the team was primed to test their new line-up, now in their second season in the Gold Division. We started out strong, winning every game, when disaster struck. Essa, our best offensive player, tore his ACL playing football for his middle school. Essa was incredibly fast and could kick the ball harder than anyone on the team, even though he was only about 5'5", 135 lbs. Though Essa was the star running back on the football team, his coach didn't even bother to call or follow up on him after the injury. I couldn't understand how anyone could just abandon one of their players after suffering a major injury, especially the coach.

Essa and his mom, Amie, had no one to help them figure out where to go to get help, so I got them a doctor's appointment with a specialist at Children's Hospital, took Essa and Amie to the subsequent appointments, and helped with making arrangements for Essa's surgery.

The surgery date set, I marked the date on the calendar. A few evenings later I got a call from Amie. She'd spoken with her father in Gambia. I ascertained that her father, Essa's grandfather, was some sort of witch doctor who claimed the surgery date wasn't a good day for the surgery because the stars and planets were out of alignment. I knew better than to argue with their beliefs, so I called the hospital and had the surgery date changed. Turned out that changing surgery dates wasn't that uncommon at Children's Hospital, as they were accustomed to helping children from around the world.

While Essa waited for the surgery date, the Mad Dogs had a home game. Essa showed up in his uniform. I asked, "Why are you wearing your uniform?"

"I want to play."

"What are you talking about, Essa? You just tore your ACL."

Mark, the assistant coach, wandered over. "What's going on?"

"Essa says he wants to play. I'm trying to explain to him that he can't, that he has a serious injury—"

Essa interrupted. "I already tore it...how much worse can it get?"

Mark asked, "You gonna play soccer on one leg?"

"Yes," the boy said. "I have a brace on, and I can still run. I've been running at the park."

"Okay," Mark said, "let's see you run."

I said, "Wait, hold up, I don't want him tearing his other ACL too."

Essa shook his head. "Not gonna happen, just watch me run," and he took off down the sideline, all this happening while the rest of the team was warming up.

Mark and I watched Essa, the fastest player on the team, run and looking as fast as ever, then discussed it and returned to tell Essa, "Okay, we'll give it a try, but if we see you limping or we think you're in any danger of getting more injured, we're pulling you out."

"Okay," Essa said, and 80 minutes later, he'd ended up scoring a hat-trick, three goals which led the Mad Dogs to an easy win.

Essa couldn't cut well, but with his north-south forward speed, he had a number of breakaways and was able to score three goals. Mark and I were both stunned. Essa was truly an amazing player, even with a torn ACL.

Essa's surgery date was a week later. I drove him and Amie to the hospital and sat holding Amie's hand through most of the three-hour surgery.

The surgeon came out to see us and assured Amie and me. "It all went well." I later arranged for the physical therapy that Essa needed.

The team was now without our top scorer with half a season ahead, but I felt that we still had enough fire power left to get the job done. The guys soon proved me right; the Mad Dogs took the Gold Division by storm, losing only one game the entire season.

In November, a month to go till season's end, we played in a Thanksgiving tournament, the "Mukilteo Turkey Shoot," featuring top teams from other recreational leagues around the region.

The Mad Dogs made it to the championship game and crushed all our opponents along the way. In the finals, we faced the first-place team from another nearby league. Again, the Mad Dogs easily won the championship game in what was supposed to be a competitive tournament. The coach of the losing team was livid and yelled at me after the game, protesting there was no way the Mad Dogs were a rec team, no rec team could be that good and that we didn't belong in the tournament. I smiled and assured him that we were indeed a recreational team and indeed that good. With the new players and their families from all these other countries, the season-ending team banquet was more fun than ever. Held at our house, the families each brought home-cooked dishes from their native country—an international feast that we all thoroughly enjoyed. The spicy Indian goat curry that Ashwin prepared was my personal favorite, but there were many tasty dishes with no one having enough room on their plates to sample all.

The following summer, the Mad Dogs played their first summer tournament. The vast majority of tournaments were only for club teams, but I was able to find a tournament in the Issaquah area that was exclusively for recreational team. The Mad Dogs won this tournament as well. The team was truly coming together and firing on all cylinders. Essa had recovered from his surgery, and he, Peter, and Tim were scoring machines. Jamal and Aaron were effective as center mid and the defense was super solid with Pemba, Yaqub, Sam, and Jeffrey manning the back line.

Mad Dogs at a summer tournament we'd just won.
The team was becoming increasingly more international.

As a way of rewarding the team for a great season, Robert and I took them to Wild Waves, a popular theme park with water slides and other thrills. Robert insisted on paying for he and his son's way, over $100.00, not small change for Robert who worked hard for his money, running a landscape company. Robert and I weren't into going on the rides, so we spent the day hanging out and watching the boys enjoy themselves. Robert has a great sense of humor, and I always enjoyed spending time with him.

After half a day at the park, Robert had to use the restroom. He returned and, having not gone on a single ride or done anything at all to get his money's worth, said in his strong English accent, "That's the most expensive shit I've ever taken."

The boys on the team were now almost 14 years old and soon headed for high school. Tim told me that his older brother, Tony, now in high school, had to leave the rec team he'd played on since he was a boy, and join a club team, because otherwise he wouldn't be able to make the high school team. I was surprised to hear this.

I told Tim I'd look into the matter. I called a friend of mine whose son had played for the local high school team. My friend told me he knew of only one boy in the past four years who played rec soccer and made the Shorewood High School team. To confirm this, I called another friend whose son played for Shorecrest, the other high school in Shoreline, and got the same answer from him.

I was shocked to discover that if one didn't play club soccer, he didn't have much of a chance to make the high school team. The high school coaches at both of the Shoreline high schools would determine the first day of tryouts which boys played club soccer and which played rec, and they would then separate them into the two groups. The rec players were barely looked at, while all of the club players ended up making the team. This was definitely not fair. Nevertheless, it was how things were.

I didn't want our Mad Dogs players left high and dry and unable to play for their high school team. I personally didn't care whether I coached rec or club, but I did care about what was best for the boys. Therefore, at the next practice, I told the boys that if they didn't play club soccer, it would be difficult for them to make the high school team.

I explained the differences between rec and club soccer and suggested the boys take a vote to decide if they wanted to continue as a rec team or become a club team. I also made clear it was a requirement in club soccer that every team hold tryouts and that no player was assured he'd make the team. Even if you're on the team one year, you could be cut the next. There were also no rules regarding playing time in club soccer, like there was in rec, where each player was required to play at least half the game. In club soccer there were times when a player would not even get into a game. Also, not to forget, the club season lasted eight months, almost twice as long as the rec season, and included summer trainings and tournaments. You had to be serious about soccer to play club.

There were pros and cons to consider for both. I mentioned the costs involved with playing on a club team, yet made it clear that if they voted to go club, I'd make sure that every player was financially able to play. "Those who can afford to should pay, and those who can't...we'll find a way to get the fees paid, maybe by holding some fundraising events or finding a sponsor. No matter how, I promise you no player will be denied the opportunity to play, if they make the team."

The team met on the side of the field without the coaches there, and discussed this for a while. They finally returned and informed me that they had voted to become a club team. This decision changed the team dynamics from that point on.

They'd soon no longer be the Mad Dogs of old. Several issues needed to be settled right away, one being a new team name. The Mad Dogs was a good name when the boys were younger, but was now too juvenile and not suitable for a club team. The local club was FC Shoreline, founded in 2001. We knew that FC Shoreline (FC for Football Club) was required to be part of the name. Once that was established, the decision was fairly easy.

Since the team was made up of many players from around the world, there should be a reference to the international makeup of our team, so we named the team, FC Shoreline International.

CHAPTER 5

THE INTERNATIONALS

There was another FC Shoreline team at the same age group, called the Jetstream—a club team that had existed for several years. This led to some controversy at the FC Shoreline board meeting about the league allowing another club team of the same age. Also, not knowing the club rules, I found I'd applied after the deadline for doing so. After much debate, it was finally agreed the club would allow for a second team at this age, if the new International club would be considered the B Team. This meant little to me or to the team, but this lower status satisfied the Jetstream coach who'd been the main opposition to the league in allowing a second team.

Since the Jetstream had already held their tryouts, the International team had to hold our tryouts as soon as possible. We were late in this process, and the season start was not far off. The date was set, and tryouts were finally held. Some of the former Mad Dogs players elected not to play, a few more than I expected. Sam, Max, and Kyle from the original Thunder-Foots moved on. Sam had friends on another rec team and opted to play with them. Max and Kyle decided they'd played soccer for long enough and didn't want to take it that seriously. They felt it was time to start enjoying other activities.

The tryouts were held with me and several other coaches and evaluators to decide who made the team. Our staff included two assistant coaches, Robert and Gary, as well as Russ and a few other soccer savvy friends.

Only two of the Mad Dogs ended up not making the team—one of the boys from China and the coach's son from the team that had folded the previous year; Josh, who'd I been nervous about adding to the team to begin with and who had been our back-up goal keeper for just the one season.

The boy from China, William, was a very nice young man, an excellent student and popular in school. He'd played with our team for only one season; previous to that, he'd played for a club team. While he was aggressive and gave his best effort, I felt he lacked ball control, was a bit awkward athletically and was often a liability on defense. His father was a Professor of Geography at the University of Washington. When informed that his son didn't make the team, he became quite upset. He met with me and let me know he felt I'd been unfair and, in his opinion, his son was every bit as good as many of the other players on the team. I told him I'm sorry, but I didn't agree; however his son was a fine young man and that it hurt me to have to make this decision. I truly hated having to cut any player, but as I explained, this was why tryouts are held and that as the coach, I had to make some difficult decisions that would not always be well received. My responsibility as coach was to put together what I felt was the best team possible and that in doing so, I couldn't allow my heart to rule my head.

I also pointed out that there were other evaluators at our tryouts who agreed with these decisions. I went on to say that we would never claim to be experts in Geography and that, conversely, he doesn't have our knowledge and experience coaching soccer. This, of course, didn't make him any happier, but it was clear nothing was going to console him, so I just ended the conversation by again saying I was sorry and then we both went our separate ways.

The team then added three new players. One was a speedster named Riyen, from Holland.

Riyen was born in a small village in the Netherlands to Nicole, his Dutch mother, and Jay, his Lebanese father. At an early age, the family moved to Lebanon because Jay wanted the family to experience the same wonderful country he'd grown up in. This proved to be a difficult adjustment for Riyen and his three brothers. They didn't speak practically any Arabic. However, soccer was part of their lives, being the most popular sport in both the Netherlands and Lebanon. The family were huge Ajax fans, Amsterdam's famous team. Searching for a team the boys could play on, the parents finally found one an hour from their home, but they had to take a treacherous mountain pass to get to practice. The coach was an older Russian man, and the soccer field was an empty sand lot strewn with sharp rocks, but the boys loved it nevertheless.

In 2000, the boys finally starting to make the adjustment to life in Lebanon, and to learning the language, when Jay and Nicole decided to move back to the Netherlands to pursue a business opportunity. After moving back, they discovered the wheels of Dutch bureaucracy posed one hurdle after another in getting their business launched. In the meantime, Nicole joined her sister and helped her run a floral and gift shop that was doing well, while Jay struggled to get his business license, the issue being mostly that he was from another country. Then 9/11 hit, and the Twin Towers fell. After this disaster, the boys started being called dirty Arabs by fellow students and were forced to deal with insults and threats on a daily basis.

They got into dozens of fights just because the other students knew they were part Lebanese. After many months of struggles in school and due to the fact that Jay still couldn't get his business license, the family decided it was probably best to return to Lebanon.

However, the return to Lebanon met with equally bad timing. Lebanon is a beautiful country and was peaceful at that time until July 2006, when all hell broke loose.

The family was living in a small village, Aley, set in the hills over-looking Beirut, when the Lebanon War began. The boys witnessed Israeli bombers flying over, filling the sky, and bombs dropping on a daily basis. They felt the ground shake and had to breathe in the smoke from all of the fires that the bombing had caused. The bombs were falling increasingly closer and closer to the Hosn's residence and the boys' school. It was clearly time to move again.

Jay had a brother in Seattle, so the family moved to the States and settled in the Shoreline area, where Riyen discovered the newly formed International team. Being from two countries, this was, no doubt, the perfect team for him.

As Nicole said, "For Riyen as well as for the rest of my boys, after struggling to fit in the Netherlands and Lebanon, finding the International team was more than just playing soccer. For us, it meant instant family."

The Hosn Family. Riyen holding the trophy with Mom, Nicole, Dad, Jay, youngest brother Julian, older brother, Alex. (Kai, the oldest Hosn brother, not shown here)

The other player added was a short but feisty and fast red-head defender. Andrew was one of the top defenders on another local rec team, the Stars.

The third to join was a tough white kid, a good athlete, though rough around the edges. JD reminded me of a younger Wayne Rooney, England and Manchester United's star player at the time.

JD had a tough homelife with two barely functioning alcoholic parents. He'd been in and out of school, but was a nice young man. I quickly saw his potential as a soccer player.

The team began training twice a week, starting in July. Later that summer, we played in our first official club tournament, the "Kick in the Grass" Tournament, held a few hours south in Puyallup. The team stayed at a hotel with a pool near the fields. It was hot, and we didn't have our first game until late afternoon. Not knowing any better at that time, I let the boys swim for a few hours and then the team met for a late lunch. It took a while to serve a group that size and the boys didn't finish eating until less than an hour or so before the game.

The game started, but we weren't ready. We played a team from Mercer Island, and our boys looked sluggish. They could barely move from being dehydrated from swimming, hanging out for too long in the hot sun, and still digesting their lunch. We got clobbered and lost the game 0–3.

I'd made mistakes, maybe even more than my share, but I was at least smart enough not to make the same mistake again. I told the boys after the game, that losing this game was not their fault. "This one's on me. I apologize for putting you in this position."

The next day, I made sure the team was well rested and hydrated, and we won both our games handily. We had now made it to the championship game, to be played the next afternoon. It was 90 degrees that day. I took the boys to a movie in the early afternoon, where they could sit and relax in an air-conditioned theater.

The same Mercer Island team that we'd lost to in the first game and who we'd be meeting again in the championship game later that afternoon was also at this same movie. Clearly, the two coaches were thinking alike.

It was a different story this time around. The game was fairly close for the first half, when midway through the second half, the Internationals got a corner kick. The kick was perfectly delivered, head-high in front of the six-yard box, when Shivy, from the left mid position, came flying through the air like he was Superman and headed the ball into the high corner of the net—as beautiful a goal as I had ever seen in youth soccer. The Internationals held on for the next 20 minutes, and we won the game, as well as our first club tournament. I'm sure our opponent could hardly believe this was the same team that they'd destroyed in the first game.

* * *

A month before the start of every season, the State Soccer Association held an annual tournament called the LPTs, which stood for League Placement Tournament. The tournament was held so that teams could compete for the level that determined which league they played in. Teams already in the leagues could move up in one of two ways. They either moved up because they'd finished in the top two places in their league the previous year or by placing high enough in the LPTs. All new teams were required to play in the LPTs to determine which level they belonged at.

There were eight different levels at that time in club soccer, starting with District Silver, District Gold, Classic also known as P5, Premier 4 aka P4, Premier 3 or P3, P2, and the top level for competitive play, P1.

A separate bracket was held for these top two levels of play in the tournament, P1 and P2. The tournament lasted two days, depending on how each team performed.

This would be FC Shoreline International's first big test as a club team. The tournament was held up in Bellingham, a few hours north of Shoreline. I rented hotel rooms for the team, three players to a room. One player, whoever drew the short straw, or in this case, the low card, slept on the floor on pillows and a sleeping bag. I usually coached the team on my own, but this time Russ insisted on coming along to help coach.

Though younger than me by 20 years, Russ had coached at higher levels than I had, including having been the high school varsity soccer coach at a powerhouse Catholic high school in nearby Everett.

The Internationals got a difficult draw for the first game, playing a high-level club team from the south end of Seattle. The Internationals gave their higher ranked opponent a real battle. The game see-sawed back and forth and finally ended in a 1–1 draw. Games couldn't end in a tie in this or most other tournaments, so the game went to overtime. The score still tied after overtime, so it came down to penalty kicks.

I was totally prepared, and had the line-up drawn out well before the tournament started. I knew who were our best penalty kickers. I kept detailed stats, and took in personality as a factor as well—which players were most calm and confident, who enjoyed the pressure and who didn't, etc.

A lot of strategy went into the decision of what order to implement when PK shootouts came about. I knew my five best penalty kickers, but in what order? Where did I want the most consistent kicker? First or maybe third? Who could best handle the pressure?

Going first might be the most pressure, unless you're going later and you needed to score the PK or your team loses. Maybe if we had a player who could hammer the ball, I'd place him first just to try to shake up the opposing goalkeeper from the get-go.

There were many things to consider in determining the line-up order, but I felt confident about the order and was fully prepared.

In the five-minute timeout, right before the PK's started, Russ asked to see the order. Upon briefly reviewing it, he argued that I needed to change the kicking order. I resisted, but he kept arguing. With time being an issue, I reluctantly agreed to the changes, and Russ quickly drew up a new order.

The new order and sudden change seemed to throw the players off. The other team ended up winning the PK shoot-out, and FC Shoreline International had lost their first game. I wasn't sure what would've happened had we stayed with the original plan, but I beat myself up for listening to Russ and not insisting on following my own plan.

A team was eliminated if it lost two games, so the next game was crucial. As luck would again have it—or in this case, not have it—out of 30-plus teams in the tournament, the Internationals would be meeting our Shoreline "neighbor" team, the Jetstream. This was not a good draw. The Jetstream had already played at the club level for several years, and a year earlier had won a state championship.

They were far more experienced and by any and all accounts, the superior team. Jetstream players and coaches, I'm sure were all thrilled with the good news—playing FCS International, a team recently up from the rec ranks, brand new to the club level.

The game started out close, but soon the Jetstream scored. As the minutes ticked by, Russ kept urging me to move our players around.

He was vocal and badgered me throughout the tense battle, even pushing me to move players into positions they'd never played before. He grew increasingly anxious and more intense as the clock wound down. The Internationals ultimately lost the game, and though it was a closer game than some expected, I was not happy.

Driving home, I tried to keep my cool and was just starting to put things in perspective, when I got a call on my car phone. It was Russ's whacky girlfriend, the same one who drove the boys crazy on their trip to Disneyland.

"Where's Russ?" she asked.

"I have no idea."

"I'm really upset!" she yelled. "Why did you ask him to coach at the tournament? We'd made plans to be together."

"I didn't ask him. He told me he wanted to come," I said, my blood pressure rising.

"I don't know where he is or when he'll be back," she said.

"I'm sorry," I said, though I wasn't. "Russ is a grown man, you'll need to talk to him."

"Fine," she huffed and hung up, leaving me to mutter, "Final straw, I'm done with him." And I was done! Russ was helpful in developing the boys' skills and enhancing their toughness, but I didn't need this additional drama. I also felt the boys had learned all they could from Russ, as had I. I called him the next day, thanked him for all his help over the years, and said it was best we now part ways.

*   *   *

Having lost both their games at the LPT Tournament, the Internationals were placed in District Silver— the bottom division. It was still club soccer, but only a step or two above the rec Gold Division. Maybe this wasn't such a bad thing after all—at least our team would likely be competitive at this level.

Needing a new trainer to replace Russ, I called the Seattle Sounders ticket coordinator and asked if any players were available to help train my team. I'd previously worked with him to place my season ticket order, and we'd established a good rapport. The Sounders, being a minor league team at the time, didn't have a multitude of fans buying a dozen season ticket seats for every Sounders home game like I was doing, and since the team only averaged about 1,000 to 2,000 fans at each game, I was clearly a valued customer In fact, so much so, that Adrian Hanauer, the Sounders owner occasionally called me to ask how I was enjoying the games and to kindly express his appreciation for my support of the team.

I personally liked the fact that the Sounders were a minor league club because it meant I could easily park right next to the stadium, sit close to the field, and still be able to watch some pretty decent soccer. Since it was the minor leagues, the players in the USL weren't paid very much. Therefore, almost all of the players had to have other jobs in order to support themselves. Many of them trained youth club teams on their off days and out of season in order to supplement their salaries.

The ticket rep called me a few days later with some great news. The Sounders' team captain, Andrew Gregor, was interested. I met Andrew for coffee and was surprised to find he was slight of build, and didn't look anything like I expected a professional soccer player to look like. Being a Sounders fan, I knew Andrew was a fierce competitor on the pitch. We hit it off and quickly came to an arrangement in which he'd train the team once a week.

The team now had the captain of the top professional team in Seattle training them.

Andrew was the center mid for the Sounders, a co-captain, as well as one of the league's top players, having made the USL All-Star team several times. And now he was going to start training the Internationals. Definitely, a coup for our team and just at the right time.

CHAPTER 6

GOING SILVER

It was fall 2006 when our team began our initial club season. Whenever we had an away game, we would all meet up at the Shorewood High School parking lot to caravan to wherever we were playing. This helped insure all the players were coming and all the parents knew their way to the game. Many of these were immigrant families, and, of course, these were the days before everyone had GPS on their smart phones or navigation systems in their cars.

I'd load up the guys in Sherri's Mazda mini-van and lead the caravan to the game. It became a tradition when we'd first start out, with me saying in my pathetic Brooklyn accent impression, "We're off like a hoid of toitles." It wasn't long before Yaqub took over and would say it instead. I brought along CDs with silly songs like an Aussie singing "Waltzing Matilda" or some Al Yankovic parodies, which the boys loved. Yaqub, though often quiet, would sometimes do impressions. He did a great Borat impression delivered with his strong Ethiopian accent, which never failed to crack everyone up.

The new FC Shoreline International team started out winning their first few games, though it was clear early on that this new club experience wasn't going to be anything like rec soccer had been. In the rec leagues, we played mostly local teams with the exception of a few tournaments. Now in club soccer, we travelled all around the Puget Sound region for our away games. One game in particular was a real eye opener.

We were playing a Hispanic team about an hour north on that team's home field. Our opponent had several dozen enthusiastic family and fans, many of whom were beating on wooden noise makers and blowing into big horns called vuvuzelas. The opposing team also had some tough-looking hombres. I later found out that two of their players had just been released from a juvenile correction facility.

With Sam having moved on, Peter was now the team's center defender. Early in the game, he was coming out to clear a high ball in the 18-yard box when one of the Hispanic players jumped high in the air, feet above his head and cleated Peter forcefully on the side of his head. Peter went down like a house of cards, knocked unconscious for a few scary moments. Back then, no one knew how dangerous concussions were and, looking back later, I realized Peter had definitely been concussed. He was out, though thankfully not literally, for the rest of that game. The ref issued a red card to their player for dangerous play.

Later on, Robert, one of our assistant coaches, noticed at half-time that several players on the other team were exchanging jerseys. We knew this shouldn't be happening. Two new players had shown up well after the ref had checked the players' cards, and they both looked quite a bit older than their teammates. In any club competition, before each game started, the rules state that the coach was required to present the center ref with player cards for all his players participating in the game. The player card had a photo, name, jersey number, and other information including birth-date and other identifying stats. The ref would match the card to the player to make sure each player was legally on that team.

If a player showed up after the game had started, the coach was required to show his player card to the ref before that player would be eligible to play.

The other team was obviously cheating, playing older players not legally on their roster. Fortunately, our International team ended up winning the game anyway. More importantly, Peter felt better later in the week and soonafter made a full recovery.

A month later, when we played that same team again, I brought along a videographer and made sure their coach saw the game was being recorded and that I was on the look-out for illegal players. The strategy apparently worked well. This time, our Internationals won without any questionable conduct from the other team.

One advantage we had over other teams was that we could communicate without the other team knowing what our guys were saying. For example, if one of our players wanted a teammate to make a run, he'd say "jao" meaning "go," in the Hindi language. Or if they wanted to let a teammate know to play the ball to the left side, they'd say, "Bajo," which meant "to the left" in Nepali. While none of the guys could speak much of their teammate's languages, they all knew at least a few choice words, many of which I wouldn't want in print.

I was naturally concerned about how the team would fare without Essa, our top scorer, but the Internationals kept on winning. We'd lost only one game all season and had one more game left to play against The Irish, whose coach was a fiery, squatty "bulldog" of a guy. The Irish also had lost only one game, so this was a must-win for the Internationals in order to secure the league title. The game started and though we were ahead by one goal; we were dominating, on the attack most of the game.

With 10 minutes left in the game, Riyen, the speedy player from Holland, was going after a 50-50 ball with the opposing goalkeeper coming to the ball. Riyen scored the goal while lightly brushing up against the keeper, the keeper initiating the contact—a sure goal in any league around the world. The referee, however, called off the goal. We all protested loudly, but there was nothing we could do. Judgement calls by the ref could not be contested. The game continued, the Internationals still up one goal when, with only a few minutes left, the Irish attacked and had two players five feet from our goal. Both players were clearly off-sides and not by a pinch. The ref again blew his whistle.

We were sure he'd blown the whistle because he'd seen their two players off-sides. Even Mr. Magoo could see they were off-sides by a "mile", at least in soccer terms. However, instead he shockingly called for a PK.

I yelled, "Two players were way off-sides. How could you not see that?"

The ref insisted that one of our defenders grabbed one of their players by the jersey.

"Which player?" I asked.

"Number 11," the ref hastily replied.

I looked at my bench and pointed to the player who wore that number. "You mean that Number 11? Our player over there, on the bench?"

The ref hesitated. "Uhh,...I meant that player," and pointed to one of Internationals' other defenders on the field.

This game was obviously fixed. Like any coach, I had faced some bad refs before. It happens in soccer, just as it does in every sport, but never before had I witnessed officiating so blatantly biased and intentionally dishonest. The Irish player took the PK kick and scored. The game ended in a tie and in regular league play at that time, there was no overtime period. The teams had now tied for 1st place. I was stunned, but hesitantly shook that coach's hand and muttered, "Some interesting calls there."

I was passionate, but I also tried my best to be a gentleman. I wasn't happy with the situation. Not at all. I refused to shake the ref's hand, as did all of the International players. I wasn't going to be a hypocrite and also felt, why honor a cheater?

It wasn't until a year or so later, that I discovered the Irish coach was a referee assigner for that area, as well as close friends with that particular ref. I found this out when we were playing in a tournament, the Sky River Tournament in Monroe. We had a guest player who was playing with our team, as is allowed in summer tournaments. We'd made it to the Semi-finals and our guest player, a very talented defender from Edmonds High School, was called for a foul late in the game. Because he already had a caution, he was issued a red-card. This second foul was completely unjustified and it meant we would lose this player for the remainder of that game as well as for the finals and we'd have to play a man short for the rest of that particular game. Immediately after the foul was called and our guest player ejected, I happened to look over on the side-lines and couldn't help but notice the coach of the Irish team looking straight at me with his arms crossed and a smug, seemingly evil smile on his face. I was shocked to even see him at this game since we weren't even playing his team? In fact, his team wasn't even playing in this tournament? However, after seeing him there at our game wearing that sardonic smile, if I had any doubts before, about our game against the Irish being fixed; I sure didn't any longer. It was now as clear as can be; he had fixed that first game as well as orchestrated this latest fraudulent call against our player and our team once again. What kind of a sicko gets his kicks by fixing a youth soccer game? That was definitely beyond my comprehension. I mentioned this upsetting incident later that day to a friend and fellow coach of another team and that was how I discovered that the Irish coach was a ref assigner for the region and that he had a reputation for being, let's just say unfair. After this travesty of a game against the Irish, I told the boys, "Although the league may show that we tied for first, we all know that's total BS.

We beat that team—we know it, they know it, and the ref ripped us off. I can't recall this ever happening before to any team I've coached, but it's clear the game was fixed. Anyway, we know we won that game and we have a better goal differential, so the Irish can think whatever they want. We are and deserve to be the one and only league champions."

The league didn't specify any of this in the standings, only showing both teams tied for 1st place. It didn't matter in the end. The Internationals were still guaranteed to move up to the next higher league next season and maybe even higher depending on how we did at the LPT Tournament.

*   *   *

In club soccer, most teams elect to play in a state tournament following the regular season. This state tournament usually starts in early to mid-January and can last as long as late February, depending on how far a team advances in the tournament. There were three state tournaments, depending on the level the team played at. The Internationals played in our respective tournament and did fairly well in our first ever state tournament, making it to the quarter-finals before being knocked out.

After the long season ended, we celebrated another successful season with what had become a team tradition, the International feast, again held at our house.

The curries, cooked by Aaron's dad, Gary, and Shivy's dad, Ashwin, were once again popular dishes, as was the Injera (Ethiopian spongy type flatbread) that one dips into a stew of spices, assorted meats, and lentils prepared by Amane. There was also a new chef "on the team," Jay, Riyen's father from Lebanon. Jay was an amazing chef and made a delicious Lebanese chicken dish accompanied with a green garlic sauce so tasty it could've been bottled and sold (which being an entrepreneur, I encouraged him to do) and with garlic so potent, you'd never have to fear vampires again...well, at least not for the next few days.

Jay also introduced a breakfast dish that became one of Sherri's and my favorites —fresh pita bread rolled up like a crepe spread with Lebanese yogurt, some virgin olive oil and sprinkled with finely chopped fresh mint and a pinch of salt.

If anyone had thought to put together a book with pictures and recipes of all the delicious dishes cooked and enjoyed by the International team families at these events, it would have undoubtedly become a best-seller.

The team played in several tournaments that summer. The first was the Starfire Xtreme Cup, at which we were runners-up, losing in the championship game. Then the Marysville Strawberry Cup, where we made it to the championship game and Jamal scored the winning goal in a penalty kick shootout. If anyone had been watching me closely after Jamal scored, they'd have noticed the tears in my eyes, no different than if one of my own sons had scored. From there, we went on to win the Snohomish Big Foot Tournament. Definitely a successful summer for our International team!

During the hot summer tournaments and even at practices, I had to keep an eye on the boys of the Islam faith, as during Ramadan, they couldn't eat until sundown. I spoke to a few of the parents to ask their guidance on what to do.

I didn't know much about Islamic religious laws, but I wanted to make sure that the boys stayed hydrated and were kept safe during the hot summer practices and games. Although even water during the day was usually not allowed, there did seem to be some kind of provision for life threatening exceptions, so I finally got the okay from all parents of the Muslim boys on the team to allow them to drink water during these hot summer workouts.

CHAPTER 7

MAJOR CHANGES AND ONE "BIG" MISTAKE!

The start of the official 2007 season began with tryouts. FC Shoreline International was required to hold joint tryouts with the Jetstream, the other FC Shoreline team at the same age group. There was one other change. Our team trainer, Andrew Gregor, had signed with the new Portland MLS team, The Timbers. He told his Sounders teammate and co-captain Danny Jackson about the Internationals, and Danny agreed to take Andrew's place in training our team. Danny grew up in the Leeds youth system in England, then came to the U.S. to play college at North Carolina, where his team won the national title and he was named National College Player of the Year and invited to the All-American team. He was the first draft choice for the Sounders, and he went on to become a perennial USL All-Star and captain of the Seattle Sounders.

Danny and I hit it off right from the get-go. He had movie star looks and a humble, soft-spoken way about him. The players quickly grew to respect and love Danny, and we all enjoyed going to the Sounders games to watch him play. He'd always be sure to come by and say hi to the guys before or after each game.

Back to the tryouts. The Jetstream was the higher-level team, and they had been together as a club team for many years. Their coach liked running the show by himself, and they didn't have a regular trainer. He did a good job with the team, as proven by his team's success over the years.

Tryout day couldn't have been more frustrating for me.

The best players all wanted to play for the Jetstream because they were the higher-level team at that time. The Jetstream planned on moving up to the P3 level, expecting to rise by performing well at the upcoming LPTs. There were a group of four excellent players trying out, all friends from nearby Roosevelt High School. All of them had played for another club that had folded the previous year.

Our International team only needed a goalkeeper and a few other players, especially a tall center back to play alongside Peter. Peter was 5'10" and had excellent timing. He was outstanding in the air, but we hoped to find a taller player to play with him in this central tandem. Patrick had been the team's goalkeeper ever since the Mad Dogs days, but he was clearly struggling as we moved up to higher levels of play. Our first season as a club team proved to me that we needed to firm up that critical position. We also lost our left-footed mid-fielder, Chip, who was a top cross-country runner and later received a scholarship to run for Western Washington University in Bellingham. Jeffrey, a top defender from China, decided he wanted to focus on tennis, so that was another spot to fill. Jeff had always seemed to lack self-confidence, yet I thought highly of him and constantly tried to get him to understand how effective a defender he was, but in the end, he decided to move on. I'd miss him and his wonderful parents, Mike and Flora, who'd been a part of the team since the Thunder-Foot days.

After watching 40-some players try out, the other International coaches and evaluators and I all agreed that three of the players from Roosevelt were the top players. I took each of them aside individually and spoke with them, offering each one a spot on our team, but each time I was rebuffed.

"Danny Jackson is our team trainer," I said. "The Sounders' Captain. Training with him will be great for your game."

I further suggested the League Placement Tournament was coming up, and they couldn't be sure the Jetstream would make the P3 level. I explained the Internationals could even end up playing at the P3 level. No one could say for sure what would happen. The Roosevelt guys still all elected to play on the Jetstream, in spite of my best efforts to convince them otherwise.

Robert, Tim's dad, having a good feel for the game, had his eye on Ethan, a big blond-haired German lad and a promising goalie. Ethan had only played rec, so I was a bit concerned, but after talking to him and watching him play, I agreed with Robert about his potential. He was clearly a marked improvement over our current goalie, so Ethan was offered a spot on the team. Ethan's parents owned the top German restaurant in Seattle, Szmania's, and Ludger Szmania was considered one of the top chefs on the Seattle restaurant scene. I'd remembered eating there several times. This also meant his parents could afford to pay Ethan's way and one less player for me to pay out of pocket.

A few of our International evaluators also had their eyes on a big defender named Jeremy. I hadn't been overly impressed watching him try out, but I knew we needed a big defender. I was never one to care much about the size of a player. In every game, we were almost always the smaller team. As I'd said to my players many times, "It's not the size of the dog in the fight, it's the size of the fight in the dog."

I reminded them that many of the world's all-time best players were not tall, including Messi, only 5' 7", as well as Iniesta, Xavi and Garrincha. Zico and Puskas were only 5' 8", as was Pele, who many still consider the best ever. Romario was only 5'5", and Maradona, another considered to be one of the all-time best, was only 5'4". However, it was usually better to have a tall keeper with a big wingspan and at least one fairly tall center back to defend balls in the air and for set pieces, such as corner kicks, both offensively and defensively.

The tall young man we had our eye on was a starter at nearby Lynnwood High School, historically not a very good team. Jeremy stood 6'3", was offered a spot on the International team—a big mistake that I wouldn't come to realize for a while.

There was one more player those on the coaching staff were all impressed with.

Musie was the smallest player at tryouts at about 5'4", 130 lbs. However, he was an excellent dribbler who kept the ball close and juked defenders right and left during the tryout scrimmages. The Jetstream hadn't even given Musie a look, and I couldn't figure out why? He attended nearby Shorecrest High School, but had only made the C team. Quite a few of the players on Jetstream were on varsity, including the coach's son, and they apparently looked down at a player on the lowly C team. I spoke to Musie and found out that his family had immigrated to the States a few years earlier from Eritrea.

We didn't have another spot on the team open, but I encouraged Musie to come to practice. Musie said he couldn't afford the club fees, and he'd been trying out only to see if he could make one of the teams.

"If you come to the practice regularly and you're as good as I think you can be," I said, "I promise you we'll find you a spot on the team and we'll pay your way as well." Musie was thrilled at this opportunity.

I later called the C team coach at Shorecrest to inquire about Musie. "He's a good little player with the ball at his feet," the coach told me, "but he's never played any organized soccer, so he's often out of position and seemed lost most of the times in our games."

That didn't worry me. Many of our players hadn't played organized soccer prior to joining our team.

I found it a lot easier to teach players where to be on the field and how to play on a team than trying to teach them basic soccer skills like how to dribble, pass, and kick.

The tryouts ended, and the Internationals had picked up two, soon-to-be three, new players with a few more on the way. The team was now practicing for the upcoming League Placement Tournament.

At the very first practice, our newly added defender, Jeremy, trying to be cool asked Essa, "Wassup, nigga'?"

Everyone at the practice immediately went silent. Nothing like this had ever happened before on our team. The boys were all furious, but none more so than Essa who, with fire in his eyes, charged Jeremy. Essa was loved by the team, but they also knew that, though small in stature, Essa was tough as could be and had a hair-trigger temper. It took three players to hold Essa back while I dragged Jeremy away by his arm.

I pointed to the far corner of the field and yelled, "Go sit over there and call your mom to pick you up."

I went over to Essa and said, "I'll take care of this. I'm really sorry. I can't believe that idiot."

I realized that Jeremy was just trying to be cool, but nevertheless, this was completely unacceptable. I was seriously thinking of cutting him right then and there, but his parents were among the nicest people one could ever hope to meet. When Jeremy's mom arrived to pick him up, I made it clear to him and to her that if anything like that ever happened again, Jeremy would immediately be kicked off the team. The next practice, Jeremy apologized to Essa and to the team. They forgave him, but that wouldn't be the last time he'd cause a commotion.

*   *   *

This time around, the LPT Tournament was quite different from last season, the first time we played in that tournament and I didn't have Russ there to screw up the results. The International team ended up with decent draws, and we won all our games. We'd now be moving up to the P4 level.

The tournament didn't go as well for the Jetstream team. They lost two games and didn't make the P3 level, the level they'd hoped and planned for. Turned out just as I'd suggested it might while trying to recruit the Roosevelt players. The two Shoreline club teams were now at the same level and in the same league.

Barely a year after turning club, the International team had caught up with the Jetstream, a club team that had been around and had been successful for many more years.

Danny Jackson, playing professionally for the Sounders, could only train the team once a week. I needed another trainer for the second practice. I knew I wasn't the best trainer myself, so I hired another trainer. There's a big difference between a trainer and a coach. I had proven to be an excellent coach, but a trainer can teach ball skills and the more technical and individual skills. Having not grown up with the game, I couldn't show the players many of the foot skills they needed to learn and develop. I could barely even kick a ball decently. I'd been impressed with a young man named Todd, who coached the JV team at Shorewood High School, where some of the players on both the International team and the Jetstream went to school. Todd also had coached a local club team that Tim's older brother played on, and he seemed to have great insight into the game.

I also decided maybe it was time for me to step back and let another coach take over. I'd done well for many years, but I thought that maybe Todd had a better read on the game and, after many seasons, it might be good to have the guys hear a new voice.

Many of the players weren't happy to hear that I'd be stepping down, but I assured them I would still be helping to coach, just not the one "calling the shots."

Right before the season start, we added two more players. One was Simon, born in Ethiopia and raised in Germany. He'd played in the Bayern Munich club system. He looked like a soccer player—slim, but sinewy, and with smooth moves.

The other player added was a tough white kid, Erik, built like a tank and fast as can be. The players would soon call him "skater boy" because of his long flowing hair and the fact he loved to ride skateboards. He was good enough to play for the Shorecrest High School Varsity, but was a rebel who didn't respond well to authority and rules. I took a chance and offered him a spot on the team. I always tried to be flexible, especially since many of the players were from different countries, but still some iron-clad rules remained, such as coming to practice regularly and showing up on time.

If a player was even a few minutes late, I'd call and ask him why he was late. It didn't take long before players made a habit of getting to practice early. The other rule didn't require much prodding from me: you were expected to work hard every minute on the pitch, whether it was a practice or a game. This last rule did not need to be enforced from me, as our captains, Peter and Tim, had established a culture for our team of hard work and dedication to being the best they could be. Peter was quiet, but highly respected by every member of our team. Tim, also well respected, was more vocal.

Each had his own style, but these two captains were a huge reason our team did so well over the years. Not just because they were extremely talented players, but also because of their strong leadership.

I didn't treat the players all the same. I realized that some came from more challenging backgrounds and didn't have the same advantages others had, so I cut those players some slack, while still being sure to explain to them why it was so important that they learn to develop the right habits.

The 2007 season started out well. The team was winning games, and everything was going smoothly, when disaster struck again. Essa was dribbling to goal when a defender ran up to tackle him. Essa made a sharp cut and went to ground, clutching the same knee he'd torn the ACL on the year before.

I took Essa and Amie to see the same surgeon who'd repaired his knee the first time around. Essa's knee was too swollen to determine the exact prognosis. The doc scheduled us to come back when the swelling went down and to set up an MRI, which soon after determined that Essa had re-torn the same ACL. This made no sense. Even the doctor couldn't understand it.

Suspecting something wasn't right, I paid a visit to the physical therapy clinic I'd set Essa up with after the first surgery. They checked their records and informed me that Essa had been to physical therapy only six times and then had stopped coming. I was completely shocked. I'd expected Essa capable of going on his own after the first few times I'd taken him. I had even called Essa often during the time he was going to PT, each time asking him how his therapy was going. Essa always told me he was doing great.

For some reason, he hadn't told me the truth. I had just assumed he'd completed his physical therapy. Had I known otherwise; I never would've let him back to play.

Once again, I helped Essa and his mom arrange the surgery, but this time I insisted Essa do everything the doctor and the physical therapist told him to do and go to all physical therapy appointments until he was cleared by the doctor. Essa didn't need any more prodding this time around; he'd learned his lesson. However, unfortunately, he learned it the hard way.

Losing Essa was tough, but as they say, one man's loss is another man's gain, so Musie, who'd been coming to every practice for several weeks and was looking sharp, was given a spot on the team.

The next game was against the Jetstream. The guys wanted this win, and I did too. The game was going okay, neither team showing much of an advantage when, late in the game, a high ball launched into the 18-yard box. Jeremy, playing center back alongside Peter, called for the ball.

Ethan, the keeper, hearing Jeremy call for it, hesitated and waited for Jeremy to clear the ball. Jeremy, however, totally missed the ball. Seen him miss it, Ethan then started to come up, but it was too late. The ball bounced behind Jeremy, where an advancing Jetstream player sprinted on to it and knocked it in the goal.

Play went on, but the Internationals just couldn't find the back of the net. We hit the post twice, we hit the crossbar a few times, but no dice or rather no goal. Jetstream had won the game. The guys were dejected, and I was too, but I praised the players. After the boys left the field, Todd and I stayed to talk about the game.

"Jeremy called for that ball and should've had it," I said. "Ethan might have gotten to it if Jeremy hadn't yelled 'I got it.'"

"Disagree," Todd said. "It was the keeper's error."

"I agree that Ethan should get to any ball he's able to," I said, "but that ball was near the 18, and it wasn't a sure thing that he could even get there."

We argued some more, but finally agreed to disagree. I went home a bit forlorn and took Moose for a walk in the reserve across the street from my house. A walk in the woods was usually good stress relief, and Moose never turned down a walk.

* * *

The International team had still lost only this one game, while the Jetstream had lost three at this point. I heard that most of the players from Roosevelt, the same ones I'd tried to woo earlier at the pre-season tryouts, ended up not coming to many practices. A few other players had stopped coming to practices altogether. The Jetstream team was obviously suffering from some player dissension.

The Internationals went on to win our next four games, when the schedule showed it was again time to play the Jetstream.

The Jetstream's goalie, Dorian, the best goal keeper in the league and the starting keeper for the Shorewood Varsity team, had broken his foot and was out for the season. We knew their backup keeper wasn't very good, so we were all pumped to revenge that first and only league loss.

Musie scored the first goal of the game. However, Jetstream soon equalized, scoring off a corner kick. The game was neck and neck. With 10 minutes to go, Jeremy got caught too high up the field and a long ball again sailed over his head.

One of our outside backs tried to get there in time, but he'd been marking another Jetstream attacker. The Jetstream's striker got to the ball and kicked it past Ethan into the goal.

The International team once again tried to equalize in the short time left, but we couldn't get the job done. We had lost to the Jetstream...once again. After the game, I told Todd, "At least part of that goal was because Jeremy was caught out of position."

"No way," Todd said. "Ethan should've had it." Déjà vu here, another difference of opinion.

"I'm not sure about that," I said, not wanting to belabor the point, "but I need to get going." Later that night, I took yet another walk in the woods with Moose, who must have loved it when our team lost, as that always assured him of a long walk.

The very next opportunity, I took our other defenders aside and asked them their thoughts about Jeremy. Our team, like most others, played the traditional flat four in the back, with two center backs, Peter and Jeremy, and two outside backs, Pemba and Yaqub, and sometimes Andrew, the redhead who subbed when they needed a break. If there were any three quieter players than Peter, Yaqub, and Pemba, I hadn't yet met them, and Andrew was certainly no chatterbox either. These defenders were skilled, but also as quiet as tongue-tied librarians.

Pemba was awarded the team-created "Golden Child Award" at one of our team celebrations, not so much because he was Buddhist, but more due to his calm disposition. "The sun is always shining on Pemba Sherpa," the boys said. It was kinda true. Pemba just had this certain aura about him. He was loved by all on our team, and he always seemed happy, calm, and collected.

In the years I coached him, I saw Pemba lose his temper only one time. It was when Jeremy was pestering him in a game a few weeks earlier. I didn't know what was said, but I could see Pemba was fuming.

As usual, Pemba seemed to have everything under control, so I stayed out of it, knowing that if Pemba was upset and Jeremy was involved, he likely had good reason.

Shy of waterboarding the three defenders, I finally got the truth out of them: none of them liked Jeremy. They all felt he was a loud mouth and that his play didn't justify his big mouth. He'd call for the ball, and then he'd miss it. Repeatedly.

One time in an earlier game, Tyler, not a starter but one of the best on our team on free kicks, was ready to launch one, when Jeremy stepped in front of him and took the kick instead. Tyler was totally pissed. Never one to be shy, he let Jeremy know so in no uncertain terms.

I watched the videotapes from the two games we played against the Jetstream and saw Jeremy call for the ball the first game and miss it, and the second game, when he was caught out of position trying to win a ball outside and far from when he should've been protecting the 18-yard area. It was clear to me that Jeremy had cost us the goals and the subsequent loss of these two games. I ran those sequences over and over and over until I was 100% convinced that Jeremy was at fault and Todd had been completely wrong in defending Jeremy. After this, I decided to take back the reins. I met with Todd and told him I was going to coach again and that he would no longer be coaching, not even helping to coach. This was a very difficult conversation, but I knew it was necessary.

I told Todd, if he wanted, he could continue to train our team once a week. Todd agreed to this, though it was doubtful that he thought I was the better coach.

Soon-after, I held a team meeting with the guys and let them know I was returning as Coach and that Todd would train the team one day a week, but he would no longer be coaching. They seemed thrilled to hear this. I also talked about our losses to the Jetstream. I never really talked much about winning and losing. It was always about effort. I explained that winning is not really something any one player can control, especially in a team sport. There is too much beyond your control. You can't control the other team, you can't even really control your team-mates. You can't control the ref, the bounce of a ball and more... All one can really control is one's own effort and one's thoughts. They just need to focus on effort and persistence. I told them never to be afraid of failure, that failure is only a temporary condition.

Then I gave them a brief history lesson on Abraham Lincoln's life.

How at age 22, he failed in business.

At 23 he ran for legislature and lost

At 24, he failed again in business

At 26, the love of his life died

At 27, he had a nervous breakdown

At 29, he was defeated for Speaker of the House

At 31, he was defeated for speaker

At 34, he was defeated for congress

At 39, he was defeated again for congress, after being elected once.

At 46, he was defeated for Senate,

At 47, he was defeated for Vice-President,

At 49, defeated for Senate again

And finally, at 51, he was elected President of the United States and abolished slavery and changed our country forever and is considered one of the greatest Presidents in U.S. history.

I loved quotes, so I would often share one or two of my favorites with the players. I finished the meeting with some words from Henry Ford, that "failure is simply the opportunity to begin again." And then from my coaching hero, the "Wizard of Westwood", Johnny Wooden, "Success is never final, failure is never fatal. It's courage that counts."

I seriously doubt these kinds of talks necessarily changed the course of our season. However, they were good lessons regardless. I suggested they not worry about the past. I explained, you can't change the past, you can only influence the future, then urged the boys to just focus on their effort and on playing the best they are capable of, aggressive, smart and unselfish soccer.

We ended up winning our next two games and every remaining game that season after I took back the reins. I'm sure our subsequent success had less to do with my talk and a lot more to do with who was being played at what position and our over-all team chemistry, especially defensively.

On that note, Jeremy, continued to be a problem. In one of our later games that season, played at Gig Harbor, Jeremy was in at Center Back, and again not playing well, so I subbed Yaqub in his place. Jeremy began arguing with me about being pulled out. I was busy coaching the team in what was a close game, so finally I said, "Just sit on the bench and keep your mouth shut." Jeremy paced around the bench, but still kept up his bickering. After trying to ignore him for a while, I'd finally had it and told him, "I'm trying to coach a game, I don't want to hear another word."

Jeremy was quiet for a short while, but then started up again. "I was playing great. Why'd you pull me out?"

"One more word and you're out of here," I said, giving him a look that could kill and pointing my finger at him.

Jeremy finally shut up, but by now, I'd decided, enough was enough.

We had two games to go in our regular season. The second to last game was in Bellevue, a day or two after it snowed. The field was icy, muddy, and sloppy. Halfway through the game, Jamal, playing center-mid, went to plant a foot, slipped on a patch of ice, and went down in pain… he tore his ACL.

Throughout my coaching, I had never had a player tear his ACL before Essa, and now we had two players tear theirs in the same season— Essa again, and this time Jamal. I helped with Jamal's doctor appointments and arranged his surgery. By this time, I was on a first-name basis with the surgeon.

One game left in the season, and the International team won. We had lost only two games all season; both of these games to our rival, Jetstream. FC Shoreline International had won the league title, while Jetstream ended up in fifth place. The International team would play in the state cup, but first we'd take a few weeks off to rest and recover.

At that last regular league game, not long after the final whistle blew, I took Jeremy aside and said, "I'm sorry, but you won't be playing for us in the state cup. This just isn't working out. You're no longer on the team."

Jeremy had tears in his eyes, and I couldn't help but feel sorry for him, but I also knew I'd made the right decision. I called Jeremy's parents, explained the circumstances, and sincerely thanked them for being a part of the team. They were disappointed, but being the nice folks, they were, they didn't argue the decision.

* * *

The team was down a few players due to injuries and less one center back, so we needed to fill some positions. The rec season still had a game to go.

I had heard about a talented German exchange student who played on a local rec team, and so I went to watch him play. The strapping German lad controlled the game and was all over the field; he was far and away the best player on the field. However, his less than impressive team lost the game.

The young man was walking off the field, his shoulders stooped in dejection, when I walked up and said, "You played well. I really like your game. I'm Skip Robbins, and I coach FC Shoreline International. Would you like to keep playing? We're a club team, and we'll be playing in the state cup in a few weeks."

Ruben didn't hesitate. "Yeah, that'd be great. I'd love to play on a good team."

Ruben was a gifted striker and exactly what our team needed. His style of play was very different from the speedy Essa, but no less effective. Ruben had played for the Bayern Munich academy team, though not at the highest level. He was a great addition to the team.

Ruben wasn't fleet of foot, but he was outstanding playing with his back to the goal.

He could put a shoulder or hip fake on the defender and get him off-balance, just for a split second, but time enough to create room to turn and shoot the ball into the corner of the net. He intuitively knew how to consistently find the inside corner of the goal.

The International team needed one more player, a big defender to replace Jeremy and improve the center back position, and I knew just the guy. Peter was a fantastic defender, the best I ever coached, but a team needed two center backs.

A few players on our team, including Tyler, my son, mentioned a friend, Max, who attended the same high school and played on the Stars, the rec team Sam had joined as well as the team Andrew had come from. Max was big, strong, a bit hefty, but deceptively quick. He explained that he wasn't interested in playing club soccer all year. He didn't want to take soccer that seriously. He was easygoing and enjoyed playing with his friends on the Stars, as he'd done since he was a little tyke. Because his rec team was now done for at least six or seven months, Max agreed to join the International team for state cup play.

State cup play began in early January, and our FCSI team won our first three games fairly easily. Ruben and Musie, both going to Shorecrest High School, bonded right away. They were a great combination, always looking for each other on the pitch. Whenever they combined, one making the pass and the other converting it to goal, they'd run to the corner flag and celebrate with a well-rehearsed jig—a fun sight for teammates, family, and fans.

Musie (# 21) and Ruben celebrating with their well rehearsed dance jig after scoring a goal

The Internationals were now in the quarterfinals and would be playing The Surge at their home field in Camas, about four hours south, not far from the Oregon border.

CHAPTER 8

WHAT A CRAZY GAME!

We chartered a bus on a cold day in late January. Parents, siblings, and friends came along to root for the team; even some grandparents joined in. On the long trip to the game, the players watched some inspirational soccer DVDs and a comedy, the movie, *Rat Race* and ate sandwiches and snacks prepared by a few of the moms on the team.

On the way to Camas to play the "Miracle Game"

The game was held in the late afternoon, on a grass field with no lights. The Surge was a decent team, but the Internationals were confident, at least until 15 minutes into the game, when the ref made a strange call resulting in the Surge getting a PK, shades of the game a year earlier against the Irish. The Internationals should have been beating this team. Maybe we hadn't yet got warmed up enough because of the cold weather and the long bus ride?

Play continued when about 15 minutes later, the ref made another unexpected strange call that again went against the Internationals.

This time the Surge was given a free kick just outside of the 18-yard box. Their player hit a high curving shot that went into the upper V and out of our keeper's reach for their second goal.

"Call the game fair! Call it fair!" I yelled, but the ref ignored me. The guys were starting to worry and so was I, but it was still the first half. I would never claim to be any Sir Alex Ferguson or even close, but I was nationally known in my industry for my marketing skills and being creative, so I came up with a plan.

There was no way I was going to just sit back and allow our team to get screwed again by a biased ref, like what had happened against the Irish team. This looked like a similar type game, where the ref wanted to control who won.

Shivy's dad, Ashwin, had brought along a video camera, but then later discovered it wasn't working properly. That didn't matter. I took Ashwin aside and asked him to act as if the camera was working fine and to stand on the sidelines and pretend he was videotaping the game.

At half-time, I approached the center ref and said as politely as possible, "Our guys came a long way, and they've worked their tails off to get to this point." Please call the game fairly. I don't mean to be rude, but I've been coaching soccer for twenty-some years and I've officiated as well. Some of these calls against us have been, let's just say, questionable. All I'm asking is that the game be called fair for both teams."

I knew how the ref would answer me, and he came through just as expected.

"We always call the game fairly," the ref huffed. "You just do your job and let us do ours."

"I understand, but please be aware that one of my closest friends is Michael Callahan. As I'm sure you know, he's the Director of Compliance for the WYSA. We have our team videographer taping this game, and if there are any more questionable calls, we'll be sending this tape to him."

I didn't wait to hear the ref's response and turned and quickly walked away.

I had no idea if there even was a Director of Compliance, but I knew it sounded official, I also didn't know a Michael Callahan. I could never be sure if this tactic was successful or not, but I do know there weren't any more questionable calls for the remainder of that game.

I gathered the guys at halftime and said, "Okay, we've had a few bad calls, but it's only half-time. We know we're the better team. Let's just go out there and put the ball in the back of the net and leave no opportunities for the game to be decided by the refs."

The game resumed and 15 minutes into the second half, the Surge scored again, this time a legitimate goal. The clock was ticking. Snowflakes were now drifting down gracefully, and dusk began to settle in, the natural light of day starting to fade and again, no lights at this field. With 10 minutes left in the game, Peter's dad figured that our team had lost, and he headed to the bus to get warm. I privately also thought the game was over, but I decided that if we were going to lose, we were at least going to go out by scoring a goal.

With about eight or nine minutes left in the game, I told the outside-mids to stay up high and not come back to help on defense. I positioned them wide, on the same line as the central striker—a modified 4–3–3 formation, but with the wingers told to stay high and not come back at all to play defense. This would of course, put extra pressure on our mid-fielders and our defenders, but we had absolutely nothing to lose at this point. I hoped this strategy would force the Surge's defensive back four to spread out and it would open up some holes in their back line.

Ruben, the German exchange student, was sent out wide on the left side, and Musie was central, playing striker. JD, the "young Wayne Rooney look-alike," was instructed to be wide right.

With five minutes to go, Ruben got a breakaway on the left and scored a goal to the far corner of the net. Still down by two goals, only a little hope remained.

With three minutes left in the game, Musie received a cross from Ruben in front of the goal and knocked it in.

The International team now had real hope, and you could see our guys' confidence building, while the Surge players were starting to look like deer caught in the headlights. You could see the panic in their eyes.

With just a minute left to go, JD hammered a ball that bounced off the Surge goalkeeper, and Musie was right there to knock it in. The ref blew the whistle soon after. The game ended in regulation time, all tied up at 3–3. The impossible had just happened...the game was going to over-time. There would be two five-minute periods; "Golden Goal," meaning the first team to score, wins. If the game was still tied after the two over-time periods, the game would then be decided by penalty kicks.

The first five-minute overtime period started. Peter, our center back, long-time co-captain and possibly our strongest player, was cramping up. We subbed Peter out, gave him Gatorade to drink, while Robert, our assis-tant coach, rubbed his leg with Icy Hot till Peter said he was ready to go back in. This happened several more times. Peter would be subbed in, and less than a minute later, would cramp up again and would have to be subbed out. He was playing on sheer guts, finding it difficult to even move. Still, Peter somehow willed himself to get back in the game.

Three minutes into the first overtime, JD got the ball, sped down the right side, beat his defender, and scored on a hard-driven ground shot that found the back of the net, just inside the far post. FC International had pulled off the greatest comeback ever witnessed by any of the players and the coaches, a game that would forevermore be remembered as "The Miracle Game at Camas."

JD putting a move on a defender

I knew right then and there: The Internationals were destined to go on to win the state championship. The trip home was one long four-hour celebration, with every player, parent, sibling, and friend still in disbelief.

Though I had coached hundreds of games and watched many hundreds more, I had never before seen a game end so dramatically. A team down by three goals with only minutes to go, and they came back to win it. Unbelievable!

In the next game, the semi-finals, we easily beat the Tusk Titans 3–0.

The state championship was held on February 16th at the pristine Starfire Stadium turf field in Tukwila. We played FC Alliance, a top club from the north end of the region. The stands were pretty full, and fans from both teams cheered on.

The team lining up before the Championship Game

The game was tight to start out, each team battling, but neither getting any true advantage. Then, opportunity knocked when Ruben, had the ball at his feet and was going to goal and was tripped up in the 18 and the ref signaled for a PK. Ruben, the most technically polished player on our team, calmly and efficiently sent his kick into the back of the net.

The Alliance then tied the game in the 2nd half and the game ended in a 1–1 tie in regulation time. This meant another "golden goal" overtime, the first team that scores wins. However, unlike the game at Camas, this game would end with a bit less drama.

Just a minute or two into the OT period, Shivy, the swift and shifty player from Fiji, got the ball on the left side and sent a cross to Ruben, who shot the ball into the net, well out of the keeper's reach.

FC Shoreline International, just two years ago a rec team, had won the U-17 Washington State Championship. This naturally led to our greatest International feast yet—a huge team celebration at our house where every player, parent, grandparent, and sibling came away stuffed, having filled their plates with delicious entrees from the many countries represented on the team. At the feast, Amie Jallow, Essa's mom, was thoroughly enjoying some delicious Jaeger schnitzel that renowned Seattle chef, Ludger Szmania (Ethan's father) had cooked up for the feast, and she inquired about the recipe. Ludger replied, "I take the pork chops—"

Amie, being Muslim, was stunned for a minute, then spat out the undigested Jaeger schnitzel, sending pork morsels flying across the room. Ludger didn't stop apologizing the entire evening. Amie, the sweet lady that she was, forgave him immediately, and they both shared a good laugh about it.

The Internationals celebrate their first State Championship

Musie and Ruben – a dynamic duo!

Pemba Sherpa, aka "The Golden Child"

Tim, Team Captain (holding the Trophy), with Dad/Assistant Coach, Robert and Mom, (Cassie) and younger brother, Simon. (Oldest brother, Tony not shown)

Essa, never one to be camera shy

Peter with his mom, Izumi and sister, Barbara

Erik, aka "Skater Boy" celebrating the big win

Essa with mom, Amie and Simon with mom, Esther

Ethan Szmania, championship goal keeper

Aaron with dad and assistant coach, Gary

Shivy, with mom, Kamni, dad, Ashwin and sister Sagrika, after his championship game winning assist

International brotherhood

Tyler and dad (Skip, coach) celebrate the win!

Jamal with his winning smile

Yaqub, aka "Yaq Attack"

International team trainers, Danny Jackson and Todd

Coach, Skip and wife, Sherri seal it with a kiss!

* * *

During the summers, many of the kids from well-to-do families on other clubs took their kids on vacation. Most International players' families couldn't afford such luxuries, so the majority of boys were available and anxious to play in summer tournaments.

The following summer, the team played in the Marysville Strawberry Cup for the second year in a row and glided along, winning the tournament championship without facing much of a challenge.

I was dropping Essa off after the long drive home from Marysville when Amie, Essa's sweet, stout mom came out to greet us. She handed me a platter stacked with something, covered in aluminum foil.

"I want to thank you for all you've done for Essa. He loves this team so much. We are all so happy and grateful to you. I don't know how to thank you, so I made you this...it's a delicacy in my country."

"Thanks, Amie," I said. "I should be the one grateful. Essa is an amazing soccer player, and all the guys on the team love him." I took the platter and placed it in my car.

I arrived home, placed the platter on the kitchen island counter, and peeled away the aluminum foil. Stacked high were dozens of fish-heads. No bodies, just the heads. Each with pairs of eyes staring up at me. I jumped back, like I'd somehow morphed into a Stephen King movie or some cheap B horror movie, like "Attack of the Killer Fish-heads", then regained my composure, pinched off a morsel of flesh from a fish-head's cheek, and popped it in my mouth. "Mmm, that isn't too bad," I muttered, thinking now at least I'd be able to tell Amie that I'd eaten some of it.

Still a bit freaked out at the sight of all those heads, I marched straight out to the back yard and heaved the entire contents of the platter over the edge of the bluff and onto the beach below. Just another day coaching the International team.

CHAPTER 9

BIG FOOT, BIG FOUL

The next big tournament was the Snohomish Big Foot Tournament, which we'd won the year before. The Big Foot Tournament was an annual summer event that many people attended in their fifth wheels and other RVs and parked at the Snohomish field complex for the tournament weekend.

Prior to the tournament, the Internationals added a few new players. One was Eamon O'Brien, starting center mid at King's, a local Christian high school, and runner-up for player of the year in his conference.

He was a strapping, stone-faced, ginger-haired young man from a rec team coached by his dad. I found it hard to get through to him at times, but understood that was often the case with players who'd been coached by their dads and especially if they'd been the best player on an otherwise mediocre team. Eamon was also a serious young man. I felt it a victory any time I could get him to smile. My only issue, other than trying to encourage him to smile, was that Eamon loved to dribble, too much so, and I tried my best to break his habit of holding on to the ball for too long instead of quickly passing it.

"I expect an offensive center mid to be the main distributor of the ball, similar to a point guard in basketball," I said and shared my respect for Magic Johnson. Magic, 6'9", had the skills of a guard but a power forward's body.

He could've probably averaged 40 points a game, but instead he chose to get his teammates involved and was always able to find the open man.

He made all his teammates around him better, which is why his college team, Michigan State, won the NCAA Championship and why he was able to lead the Lakers to five NBA Championships. Being unselfish with the ball won Magic three MVP awards and a starting position on the NBA All-Star Team 12 times. What I want is for you to make everyone around you better. That's how a great center mid plays the game. If you're dribbling the ball and your teammates are making great runs to get open and you don't reward them by passing them the ball, what do you think will happen? Put yourself in their shoes. They're making long runs, and you're still holding on to the ball, and you keep dribbling another 10 yards. What do you think is going to happen if our mids are making these runs, and you're rarely passing them the ball?"

Eamon lowered his head and just stared down at the pitch and said nothing, so I said, "I'll tell you what will happen. They'll stop making those runs, and then our team is screwed."

I had more than a few conversations like this with Eamon, but he still had the propensity to dribble or try to score himself, though I did see an improvement as time went on and he learned to better trust his teammates.

The opening day of the Snohomish Big Foot Tournament, the International team started out well, winning our first two games. Sherri was out of town for a few days. Knowing I might get home late, I gave Moose a bowl filled with chicken leftovers, including some skin and fat. After returning home after that long first day, I walked through the door, only to discover that Moose, unable to get out into the yard, had crapped all over the living room carpet. To make matters worse, the chicken gave him the runs. It would be a polite understatement to say, it was a disgusting mess.

I plugged my nose and searched the house for rags and cleaning solution and spent hours cleaning up the smelly disaster before Sherri got home. Next morning, I went to the local hardware store and rented a carpet steam cleaning machine to make sure the carpet was spotless. Finally, when it was all cleaned up, I left for the tournament.

I got to the field and ran into Ethan's mom, Julie, and sighed, "Jeez, I'm exhausted. Moose crapped all over our carpet, and I spent half the night cleaning it up."

Julie raised her eyebrow. "Huh, what...? Musie crapped on your carpet?"

I laughed. Julie thought I'd been talking about Musie, the talented Eritrean player on our team. "No, I mean...Moose, our dog."

Julie and I couldn't stop laughing.

That day our team made it to the tournament semi-finals and would face the top seed, Snohomish United—a successful club with a reputation for having big and tough farm boys who played hard. Some might even say, dirty. They were also at the Premier 2 level, two levels up from where FC Shoreline International had played last season. There was no question who the favorite here was. Snohomish was the host team and had many fans to cheer them on.

Some friends of the Snohomish United players had even dragged a beat-up sofa to within a few feet of the sidelines, so they could have "front row" seats and cheer their buddies on.

Within the first fifteen minutes of the game, Musie, 5'4" and 130 pounds, juked Snohomish United's biggest player with some cheeky dribbling moves and scored a goal close to where the defender's friends sat on the sofa. The defender was not happy being so humiliated, especially right in front of his friends. The game continued when Eamon, the new ginger for International, dribbled past three defenders and scored. The Internationals were now up two goals to nil.

I didn't mind that Eamon dribbled to score the goal since he was in the 18-yard box. I wanted him or any of our players to go to goal and try to score whenever the opportunity presented itself.

As the clock wound down, the Snohomish players became increasingly frustrated, and began knocking into any International player with the ball. Hit numerous times, the Internationals started one touch passing the ball, so the ball was already gone by the time a defender came near. The guys, tired of being bashed, knew they couldn't depend on this ref to make any calls. Out of fear of being hammered, the FC Shoreline Internationals were playing some of the best soccer they'd ever played.

This is how the top teams in the world play. One of the best examples being Barcelona with Messi, Xavi, and Iniesta and how I always wanted and helped train my team to play, with quick one and two touch passes, moving the ball faster than an opposing defender could possibly move. Obviously, we'd never come close to duplicating the quality of play of a world class team like Barcelona, but great passing is a quality that any soccer team wants to continue to develop and work towards.

With 10 minutes left, the Internationals up by two goals, Musie got the ball. The same defender who Musie had scored on earlier in the game was on him again, helplessly attempting to defend him once again.

Part of the strategy in soccer if your team is up and the game is winding down, is to have the player with the ball shield out the defender and do his best to milk the clock for as long as possible. Having the best ball control on the International team, as well as a low center of gravity, Musie was able to prevent the big defender from getting to the ball.

The longer Musie shielded the defender out, the more that defender got frustrated. Once again, the big defender's friends were sitting and laughing at their big bruiser friend allowing a tiny guy like Musie to prevent him from getting the ball.

After he tried everything else to get the ball, the big defender began shoving and grabbing Musie, using his hands, kneeing him in the back... the ref could have and should have called at least a dozen fouls by now. Instead, the useless Ref just stood inside the center circle some 30 yards away and continued to watch. The big kid, finally in a fit of frustration, threw Musie down to the ground and jumped on top of him. Musie was now being crushed by a six-foot-tall defender who outweighed him by 60 or 70 pounds. This was one of those instances when time seemed to stand still. The young ref hadn't even moved from the center circle, offering no more help than a mannequin in a department store. Musie's face was now buried in the grass. He was flailing his arms, trying his best to get up and out from under this big lug, but with the size of this defender, it was virtually impossible for him to move.

Breaking the long silence, one International mom finally yelled, "Musie can't breathe! Musie can't breathe...someone do something!"

I saw Musie gasping for air with this big immovable man mountain on top of him, continuing to flail his arms, trying to get out, but as helpless as a midget wrestler in a Hulk Hogan hold. By this time, it was clear I had to do something. Coaches are not allowed on the field unless waved on by the ref, but this ref was absolutely worthless. Finally, seeing no other choice, I ran out on the field, got behind the big defender, and grabbed him by both of his shoulders and pulled this big defender off Musie.

I'm about 5'8" and 165, and this big kid towered over me and had at least 40 pounds on me. I fell back, the defender fell back with me, and we both landed on the ground near one another. Musie was free at last and able to breathe. Now I expected the big kid to come after me, but fortunately that didn't happen.

The boys on the sofa then started an altercation with a couple of the players on the Internationals bench. Several punches were thrown, but the fray was over in a flash. The ref finally ran over and issued a red card to the big Snohomish defender, as deserved. Then shockingly, he red-carded

Yaqub, who hadn't even been involved. Several players on the Snohomish team told him it wasn't Yaqub...it was the little guy. Realizing his mistake, the ref then red-carded Musie instead.

"What the.... our player was attacked by their defender!" I yelled. "He didn't do a thing."

The ref ignored me, just as he'd ignored calling any fouls the entire game, and he scurried off the field and away. The Shoreline International team had won the game, and we now had to get ready for the Tournament Championship game, scheduled a few hours from the end of this crazy game. I now had to go to the tournament trailer to meet with the officials, to get Musie's red card rescinded, so he'd be able to play in the championship game. I figured this wouldn't be a problem. I entered the trailer and introduced myself to the tournament officials and carefully explained to them exactly what had happened: that Musie was attacked and taken down and he hadn't done anything to provoke the attack, other than adeptly control the ball.

The officials listened, asked me a series of questions, and told me to return in half an hour for their response. When the thirty minutes had passed, I returned to the tournament trailer, confident the officials would make the proper and obvious decision.

The officials then informed me that because Musie had flailed his arms and thrown his elbows out, that the red card would stand.

"That's ridiculous. Our player was physically assaulted by that big defender, and he hadn't done a single thing to justify this attack. This is grossly unfair. It's clear and outright bias. We've played in this tournament for three years, but I'll make damn sure my team never plays in another Snohomish Tournament."

I angrily started back to where my team was gathered when, to add insult to injury, I now see the Snohomish coach running towards me. The pudgy little Brit starts yelling at me. "I'm going to see to it that that's the last f...ing game you'll ever coach." Now I'm beyond being frustrated and angry, I'm infuriated. I quickly gave chase and, seeing me coming at him, he immediately turned and started running away. I continued to chase after the now frightened Brit, no longer caring about any repercussions. Though I'm not the sort to instigate a fight, I was ready to beat the living crap out of this mouthy little bastard.

However, the little Brit scurried off like a scared rabbit. Finally, coming to my senses, I ceased chasing him, realizing it just wasn't worth it.

I joined up with my team, and we sat around in the shade waiting for the championship game to start when a Snohomish police officer walked over and asked, "Who's the coach here?"

"That'd be me, Officer. I'm Emerson Robbins. I coach FC Shoreline International."

The officer paused, thinking... then asked, "Emerson Robbins of EE Robbins?" I was one of the top radio advertisers at that time on many of the Seattle stations, and since I voiced my own commercials, I was well known to pretty much anyone under 40 years old who lived in the region.

I hesitantly answered, "Yes?" and the officer said, "I bought my engagement ring from your store a few months ago."

We both chuckled a bit at this, and I proceeded to tell the officer what had happened.

The officer said, "I'm really sorry about this, but several Snohomish fans are claiming that you assaulted their player, who happens to be a minor."

"What? That's insane!" I said and again explained what happened in even more detail. I was completely stunned—how could anyone think I'd assaulted that kid, when everyone could clearly see that all I'd done was pull him off Musie? I was now being accused of assaulting a minor, not a minor charge. I'd never been in any kind of trouble except maybe a few speeding tickets. This was a shocking and potentially serious situation.

The officer seemed to believe my end of the story and possibly even sympathized, but said, "We won't be making an arrest at this time, but you should be aware there will likely be charges filed soon."

Our now frazzled International team went on to play the championship game, but unfortunately without Musie.

It was a close game, but the Internationals lost in the last few minutes when Andrew missed heading out a ball and an attacker ran on it and scored—the first time the Internationals had lost a championship game. I didn't care much about the result. It had been a long, difficult day, and at this point, I just wanted to head home.

The following week, I received papers requiring me to go to the Snohomish Police Department.

I researched and subsequently hired one of the top defense attorneys in the State of Washington, a near Johnny Cochran doppelganger, and a few days later, met with him at his offices in downtown Seattle. The attorney listened to the story of what happened and then referred me to one of his associates, as this wasn't exactly the OJ case, or at least not a big enough case for him to handle personally. He also introduced me to one of his private investigators.

Since a law firm of this level doesn't come cheap, I had to pay the firm a $5,000 retainer. Later that week, my attorney went about obtaining sworn statements from players and parents from the International team who'd attended the game and witnessed the events. They were all equally shocked and upset that I was being accused of assault. I soon-after had to make several trips to the Snohomish Police Department, accompanied each time by my attorney.

The matter dragged on a few more weeks and resulted in many sleepless nights until I was finally informed that the other team's parents had elected to drop all charges, likely realizing they didn't have a leg to stand on.

Learning from this traumatic incident, I tried to have a videographer attend and tape every one of our games. I was now out five grand, and our team had lost the championship game.

Maybe the only positive outcome was that even though there was little doubt before, every player and parent on the team now knew I would always have their back and, in Musie's case, quite literally.

Another benefit of this stressful event was that Musie, after spending so much time together and speaking in detail about the incident, allowed me to learn more about Musie's life and how he happened to come here from Eritrea.

I found out that Musie had emigrated to the U.S. when he was 12 years old. There'd been a bitter and bloody war between Ethiopia and Eritrea from 1998 to 2001, and Musie and his family fled to Sudan. Musie remembers the bombs falling as he was tending the family's flock of sheep, and he remembers he and his family having to take refuge in the woods for several weeks to escape and stay safe from the bombings.

The family finally fled to Sudan, leaving their home and loading all of the belongings they could fit into a donkey driven cart. Then, only a few months after arriving in Sudan, Musie's father was suddenly accused of being a spy for Eritrea. Musie's father was absolutely not a spy, but Sudan was 97% Muslim and Musie's father and family were ardent Christians, so he wasn't believed.

Once again, the family was forced to escape, this time back to Eritrea where, a year later, he sought political asylum for the family in the U.S. After a long and stressful wait, the family was finally allowed to emigrate to America in 2004. Musie's father still bears animosity towards Ethiopians, as his brother and five other family members were killed in the bloody war.

Musie, having been in the U.S. for only a year when he joined the Internationals, had never played on an organized team before. Invited to join the International team gave him a strong sense of pride, quality training with a professional player, equipment he'd never had before including uniforms, cleats, the whole experience of being on a team complete with back-packs, team jackets, meals paid for, flying to tournaments, staying in hotel rooms...being on the Internationals changed his life and dramatically boosted his feeling of self-worth. Musie said after joining the Internationals, he felt like a professional player and that being on FCSI changed his life and helped to give him tremendous self-confidence. He became good friends with Jamal and Yaqub, the brothers from Ethiopia.

They shared a true friendship, even though their native countries had fought a war against one another. Musie saw that everyone could live together in peace and harmony in America, and this made him love his newly adopted country even more.

Musie after winning the first State Championship

CHAPTER 10

REVOLVING DOOR

The 2008 season brought more big changes; the Jetstream team was folding. After the team failed to make the P3 level at the LPT Tournament, some of the Roosevelt players who'd spurned my offer to join our International team at tryouts, ended up flaking and stopped coming to the Jetstream practices. A few even quit the team. This was one of the problems with the club tier system. When a team didn't qualify for a higher league, some of the more ambitious players would occasionally "jump ship" and abandon their team to join a team in a higher-level league.

The moral of this story for me was, "Be careful what you wish for." In other words, though I tried to coax the Roosevelt players to join the International team at the tryouts, I was now very relieved they had turned me down. I didn't want players who were just out for themselves and had no loyalty to their team.

I still felt sorry for the Jetstream coach and team—around for so many years, this is how it ended. I had been looking forward to beating them without Russ or Todd coaching. The Jetstream had been the top club in our area and early on, the standard that I wanted my team to aspire to. However, in less time that I could have anticipated, I felt we had become the superior team. This past season, when we were at the same level, in fact, the same league; we became League Champions and the Jetstream finished near the bottom of the league. Nevertheless, The Internationals had never beat the Jetstream in three tries and now we never would.

There were a few players on the Jetstream I hoped would join the Internationals. At the top of the list was Charley Newman who attended Bishop Blanchet, a local Catholic high school, the same school as Ethan, the International team's goal keeper. I had a good rapport with Charley.

Whenever I'd see him, I'd say, "Hey, what's up Charley Hustle?"

Charley would smile that great smile of his and say, "Hey, Coach."

Charley wasn't one of the Jetstream's star players, but I felt he got a raw deal. I loved players like Charley who always played his heart out. One time, at a tournament, after a game, I saw Charley sitting on a bench, his kneecap swollen to the size of a grapefruit.

"Whoa, Charley, what the heck happened?"

He just shrugged. "No big deal. Just needs to be drained."

I was alarmed looking at the elephantiasis-sized knee cap, but to Charley it seemed to be nothing more than a hangnail. Charley was a tough guy, and yet as nice a guy as you'd ever ask for.

One day, at our practice, Charley came over and asked, "Hey, Skip, I guess you heard the Jetstream folded; I'm wondering if I can join your team?"

"Absolutely, Charley Hustle. I'd love to have you join the Internationals."

He fit on the International team as if he'd been there from the very start. He won over every player on the team in no time at all. In fact, it wasn't long before he was named a captain along with Peter and Tim. Charley filled the team's need for a center back, though he'd played outside back most of the time on the Jetstream. However, I knew he'd make a great center back, and he most definitely did.

Charley's cousin, David, also asked to join the International team. His father was born in Spain. Soon to be nicknamed "Kue," David had been the starting striker for the Jetstream.

Like his cousin Charley, he was a likeable young man and a talented attacker. Kue played for a top Catholic school, O'Dea in the Capitol Hill area of Seattle. He was another good addition to our team.

One more Jetstream player asked to join the International team, a defensive mid, a tall, lanky young man named Nate. He started for the Shorecrest varsity team and now needed a new club team. Nate was both a skilled and a team player, so he was also given a spot on the team. All three of these players were also able to pay their own way, which was an added bonus that I naturally appreciated.

Around this same time, Erik, aka "Skater Boy," while skating through a crosswalk one day after school, was hit by a school bus. Erik flew high up in the air and landed on the concrete about 20 feet from where he'd been hit. He was rushed to the hospital. I heard about the accident the very next day, when I received a call from Erik's mom.

"Erik's lucky to be alive," she said, "but he won't be playing soccer again, at least not for a very long time. His femur bone is broken, and he has several torn ligaments."

"I'm so sorry," I said, "is there anything I can do?"

"That's okay," she said in a trembling voice. "My boy is alive, and the doctors expect a full recovery, but maybe you could help out with a hospital bed for when he comes home? We need one that raises and lowers, and I just don't have the money for it right now."

"I'll take care of it," I said and ordered one to be delivered the next day, ready to comfort Erik when he returned home from the hospital.

Erik, though an undisciplined player, was tough, strong, and fast. He had potential, but because he wasn't much for rules and didn't like being told what to do, he never played for his high school team.

Had he wanted to; he'd have definitely made the powerhouse Shorecrest varsity team. Although not the easiest player to coach, I understood he was a free spirit, so I always cut him some slack. Erik's natural position was defensive mid, similar to a free safety in football, but he didn't like being restricted to one position on the field and have to do the dirty work, or at least so he felt. He wanted to score and get the glory, but when he played, anything could happen. I remember one particularly impressive goal he scored. He and one of his teammates had a two-on-one against the opposing team's goalie. Erik had the ball and was dribbling to goal when he pointed and called out to his teammate, as if he was going to pass him the ball. I can't recall who our other player was, but I do clearly remember that the goalie fell for the fake and started toward Erik's team-mate and Erik calmly took the shot into the now half empty goal—a brilliant goal.

Even the jersey number Erik picked, #91, was unconventional...that was Erik. Nevertheless, he'd played an important part in the International team's first state championship and would be missed. Many of the boys on the team went to visit Erik when he returned home from the hospital. I had patches made up with #91, and the boys wore them on their sleeves for the remainder of that season.

A few more changes were in the works. Simon, the young man from Ethiopia, who, like Erik, had played on the 2007 state championship team, chose to forsake soccer and focus on his music.

He was an aspiring rapper and totally consumed with becoming a star.

I was saddened by the news, as I'd become close with Simon and had tried to be a positive influence in his life.

I remembered the time when Simon needed a ride home from practice, not long after joining the team.

I asked him about his background, and Simon said that he and his family were born in Ethiopia but they'd moved to Germany when he was a small boy. A few years after arriving in Germany, his father, a doctor, fell in love with another woman and soon after divorced Simon's mother. His dad moved to London with this woman, whom he later married, and they started a new family. Simon tried to contact his father several times, as recently as last year, he told me, but his dad didn't want anything to do with Simon because he was worried about upsetting his wife and shaking up his new, second family.

Simon wept. "How could my father not even care about me, his own son?"

Holding back my own tears, I had no answer but finally said, "I'm so sorry, Simon. I only wish your dad could know what an amazing son he has. Maybe someday he will. Thank God, you have such a wonderful mother."

That was all I could think of saying, but I never forgot that moment and how Simon's heart was broken and that he might never fully heal from being rejected by his own father. I understood that Simon was no longer interested in playing soccer, that he wanted to focus on his music. Sad to see Simon leave, I had no choice but to accept his decision. We hugged, and I wished him great success with his music career.

Later on, Simon gave me a CD of his music and, though I'm far from being a music expert, I was definitely impressed. We stayed in touch, and Simon even came to watch his former team play a few times.

Simon with his mom, Esther

Though sorry to lose these boys, I wasn't overly concerned about our team losing a few players. We had enough new players to fill Erik's and Simon's spots. I also felt the new players were probably even an upgrade as they were more dedicated to soccer. Therefore, though sad to lose these players, I knew this was likely a net gain for the team. The roster, however, would see even more changes.

Bill Wilkins, a good friend of mine, who coached a nearby club team of the same age, the Evergreen Cyclones, called and said, "Hey, thought you should know my team is folding."

"What...why?" I asked. "You guys are really good."

Bill chuckled. "I guess, though your team beat us twice."

"True," I said, "but you have a lot of talented players and you're a great coach."

"Thanks," Bill said. "Now I need to find a new team for Jacob...what do you say? Eric, our keeper, also needs a new team. He's an excellent goalie, he was All-League for his high school team. And also, you know Stuart; he's a solid outside back."

I was definitely impressed with Bill's son, Jacob, a mid-fielder for Shorewood High School and a really nice young man. I could also use another goalie. I had felt that one reason Bill's team may not have performed to their full potential was because of three particular players on that team. Considered top players, they were also each head-strong and, I would guess, difficult to coach.

"I'm not really sure Stuart will fit in," I said, "but I'll give him a shot if that's what you want."

"Much obliged," Bill said, "I hope they're a good fit."

I was hesitant to add so many new players, even though they were talented, but Bill was a good friend and he'd helped me through the years with advice, so I didn't feel I could turn him down.

The Internationals had added six new players and were ready to play at the P3 level, the third highest level in premier youth soccer. Unfortunately, this would also be the highest level we'd reach because the Washington State Youth Soccer Association had done away with the League Placement Tournament, thus, the International team wouldn't get the opportunity to move up the next season. This could also turn out to be our final season as a team, since many of the boys were now seniors in high school.

The state association made an even bigger change. The top Premier levels were going to be re-named and re-formatted, and these leagues would now only be made available to the largest, and most prestigious clubs in the state.

These clubs had likely used their strong influence to pressure the state association to limit the top premier levels to this select group of larger and more prestigious clubs. These big clubs didn't like their teams exposed to possible relegation by smaller, independent, no-name club teams. They knew that this would adversely affect their brand. Youth Soccer Clubs had become big business.

Many of the directors of these larger clubs were now pulling in size-able salaries because of how many teams and players their club had. The player fees were anywhere from about $2,000 up to $5,000. and more. The more players they could attract to their clubs, the more ka-ching.

Thus, these top clubs in the state formed an exclusive league that only teams from their clubs could play in.

FC Shoreline, the International team's parent club, was a relatively minor club and, like several dozens of other clubs around the state, wasn't invited, welcomed, or allowed to join these high-level premier leagues.

I didn't care, nor did the players, at least the core players who'd been with the team for years. Maybe some of the newer players may have cared, but if so, I never heard any grumblings The International players just enjoyed playing the game. Having so many players from other countries, we'd developed a team culture where players were just grateful to have the opportunity to play. The guys never seemed to care or worry at all about what level they played at...they just enjoyed playing the "beautiful game."

Maybe the players felt these issues worked out anyway, since our International team had moved up to a higher level almost every year we'd played, going back to the Mad Dogs days. The Internationals had confidence they'd continue to be successful.

CHAPTER 11

SUBTRACTION BY ADDITION?

The team, now loaded with new and talented players, entered The Copa Del Mar Cup, a high-level tournament in San Diego, where we'd be playing some excellent teams. With the added firepower, the Internationals looked forward to the test. Not all of the players were able to make the trip, but most of the original lineup made it, plus several of the new additions to the team.

The team was at Sea-Tac airport, getting ready to board their flight to San Diego, when a TSA official approached and asked, "Who's in charge of this group?"

I stepped up. "I'm the Coach. Why do you ask? Is there a problem?"

The official said, "Yes, I'm afraid so. One of your group is on the No-Fly list."

I thought to myself, it had to be one of our Muslim or Hindu players or, if not one of them, one of our African players. "Can you tell me the name?"

"Yes, Eamon O'Brien."

I chuckled and pointed Eamon out—a red-haired, pink cheeked, All-American boy. The official asked Eamon a few questions, and the matter was soon resolved. Apparently, there was an Eamon O'Brien in the Irish Republican Army who was on the No-Fly list. The TSA officials realized the IRA O'Brien was at least 50 years old and clearly not this ginger-haired American high school boy headed to play in a youth soccer tournament with his team.

* * *

In our first game, the Internationals faced a U19 team based out of San Diego. They were a year older, their players all Hispanic and looked like they were professionals, or so I thought while watching them warm up before the game. We were facing a major challenge, and I couldn't help thinking to myself, *what have I gotten us into?* I then noticed all three refs were also Hispanic. Not necessarily a good omen.

The game began, and it became clear very quickly that this was by far the best team the Internationals had ever played. The game wasn't five minutes in when the other team was awarded a corner kick. Yaqub was marking the far post, and his hand was holding the post when the ball flew in and hit his hand. Yaqub hadn't moved his hand to control the ball, but this was a judgment call, and the ref red-carded Yaqub and called for a PK. Now we'd be playing a man down against the best team the Internationals had ever played.

The opponent scored the PK and then added three more in the next 20 minutes. They were one and two-touching the ball, moving it with speed and precision and launching "rockets" from as far as 35 yards out. The game was turning into a joke. The International team had no business even being on the same pitch with these guys. This team would've beat any youth team in the State of Washington. In fact, I'd bet they could've beat most college teams.

The score five nil, my mental state transitioned from worry to serenity and even, awe. I soon found myself able to just watch and enjoy this extraordinary team play.

The game ended. We shook our opponents' hands, graciously and complimentary, as did they.

Though the Internationals were destroyed like never before, losing the game six nil, we all appreciated our opponents' skills.

The guys also recognized the other team kindly took their "feet off the pedal" after a while and only played their subs rather than trying to run up the score. I spoke with their coach and was very complimentary, which wasn't difficult for me, given how impressive they were.

I wasn't anxious to play another game, but we'd made our bed, so now we had to sleep in it. The Internationals got ready for the next game, only a few hours away.

As it happened, that first team turned out to be, thankfully, an anomaly. The rest of the teams we played were more evenly matched with our team.

As expected, the Hispanic team that had crushed us that first game ran away with the Tournament Championship. However, what was not expected was our International team ended up winning all our remaining games and came away with the consolation championship—definitely an unexpected result after that initial onslaught.

Before heading down to Southern California, I asked my brother Steve, who lived on the beach in Laguna, if I could bring the team to visit and swim in their pool and enjoy the ocean. Steve and his wife Marisa, my beautiful Italian sister-in-law, kindly welcomed the team, with the provision they stay outside. I understood not wanting this wild band of testosterone-driven teenaged boys tromping through their beautiful home, once owned by Ricky Nelson, the famous teen heart-throb who perished in a plane crash several decades earlier. The house, or rather, the estate, was on three levels, over 10,000 square feet, and built into the side of a mountain.

A few years after I sold out and left the company, Steve had expanded the company, sold out to a venture capitalist, and made a bloody fortune.

I was happy for my brother and grateful we were able to remain close. Their property was situated on an amazing beach.

A waterfall on their property cascaded off the mountain into a rock swimming pool below. The house had two elevators, six bedrooms, six bathrooms, two kitchens, two wine cellars, numerous staircases, a koi channel that surrounded almost half the house, a billiards room, a theatre, a gym, an inside jacuzzi as well as one outside, a sauna, and all of the ocean toys one could ever dream of—kayaks, paddle boards, snorkeling gear, you name it... To top it off, this magnificent estate was located on a white sand beach adjacent to a surrounding marine preserve teeming with all types of colorful fish, lobsters and other assorted sea-life. None of the boys had ever seen a home like this, especially those from other countries. Even very few Americans had ever seen a place like this, at least, not up close.

The guys had a day they'll never forget, swimming in the pool, sliding down the pool slide, body-surfing, kayaking, soaking in the hot tub, and more. Steve and Marisa were gracious hosts. Marisa, being a gourmet Italian cook, served the motley group of boys a delicious lunch.

* * *

Following the busy summer, the team took a month off to rest and recover, but it wasn't long before the guys were chomping at the bit to get back on the pitch. There'd be no LPTs this year or even joint tryouts, since the Jetstream, the other FC Shoreline team at this same age level, had folded.

The biggest problem the team would face this season was one many teams would love to have—too much talent. While seemingly a good thing, having so much talent made it difficult for the players as well as for me, the coach.

Most of the players were starters for their respective high school teams and weren't used to coming out of the game, and if they did, not for long. There was no way I could possibly find enough minutes for all of them. Some players would not be happy.

In soccer as well as other team sports, a player needs time to get into the flow of the game. Players also need the experience of learning one another's tendencies in order to establish continuity. Playing in sync may be more essential in soccer than in any other team sport, which is why many consider soccer the ultimate team game. A world-class soccer team can be compared to a great symphony orchestra in which every musician has mastered his part and performs as one unit in harmony with the orchestra. If one instrument is off-key or out of sync, the entire performance suffers. No different with a soccer team.

Establishing continuity with all these players would be close to impossible. I'd clearly been too generous in agreeing to take on all the new players from the two teams that folded. As a result, a third of the way into the season, Aaron, one of our two players from Fiji, who'd been with our team ever since the Mad Dogs days, said he wanted off the team. He wasn't getting the playing time he felt he deserved and so he'd joined a top P1 team, Emerald City FC that was looking for players. A player switching teams once the season had started required the coach to approve the release of the player. I understood Aaron's frustration and didn't blame him at all.

I felt badly losing a player who'd been such an integral part of the team for so long, but I also felt that Aaron, though a good center mid, was not as effective defensively as Jake or Nate, nor as effective offensively as Eamon and Musie.

My job as coach is to do what's best for the team—not playing someone because I liked him or because he'd been with the team for a long time. It was my responsibility as coach to play the players who put our team in the best position to win.

I cared about Aaron and therefore didn't hesitate to sign his release. We hugged, said our farewells, and Aaron was off to join his new team— the first and only time our International team had a player voluntarily leave for another team.

Tyler had already been unhappy with his playing time, as well as with me, his dad. There were games where I didn't play him at all, and a few more when he only got in a game for 10 or 15 minutes. Tyler had some excellent skills, and was one of the top players on free kicks and PKs. He also had very good vision of the field, passed the ball extremely well, and would always bring energy and enthusiasm to the game, yet he could also be a defensive liability at times. He was extremely tough and tenacious, but he had a tendency to over-commit. Fast going north and south, Tyler wasn't as skilled as many of our other players were in controlling the ball on the run. He hadn't played high school soccer, as most of the other players had. He worked as hard as anyone at our practices, but would rarely put time in on his own. Most of our players were out on the field whenever possible, working on their game.

I explained to Tyler, my responsibility to the team. A dad at home but a coach on the field, it wouldn't be right for me to treat my son differently than any other player. When the subject arose, I said, "If you want more playing time, you need to earn it by working on your game and improving those areas that your coach tells you needs improvement." And if you don't want to do this, maybe you should consider joining the Stars, like Sam did."

Naturally, telling him this hurt me deeply, but I also knew I needed to tell him the truth for his own benefit. It's an important lesson for any parent to teach his or her children. If you want something in life, you have to be willing to work for it. No one is going to hand you anything once you're on your own.

Tyler had quite a few friends on the Stars. Guys who played for the sheer fun of it and had no interest in taking soccer too seriously. Maybe that's where Tyler would best find his place, but I knew this wasn't my decision to make. There were times I asked myself if I was doing the right thing? Shouldn't I be looking out for my own son? However, I'd seen teams coached by fathers who unfairly favored their own son and it created resentment among the other players and among many of the parents as well. I also felt I had a responsibility and commitment to our team. Many, if not most of the players on our team wouldn't have been able to play Club soccer at all, if it weren't for my helping to sponsor and coach them. I also knew I was helping many of them outside of soccer as well, hopefully teaching them some life lessons and serving as a mentor to some of the players, who didn't have a father or a decent role model in their life. I decided, that fighting for playing time was up to him. He needed to earn the time, not have me hand it to him just because I was his father. Maybe I was overly tough on him? I could never be sure? However, I did know I'd prefer to error on being overly tough as his coach, rather than show any undue favoritism. I do wonder if it's best if fathers coach their son or daughter for a year or two, possibly three and then step away and let their child be coached by someone else. The relationship with one's child is too important to take any chances with and it definitely complicates the relationship if you're trying to be both a coach and a father.

This problem was also the result of our team becoming stronger every single year. The players on the International team were, by now, all excellent, highly motivated soccer players. Most were varsity starters for their respective high schools; quite a few were All Conference players. Many would go on to play soccer in college. It wasn't easy to earn playing time on the International team. This was an issue that would never be fully resolved. Tyler and I, father and son, loved each other, but on this, we didn't see eye to eye. Sherri, a loving mom, usually sided with Tyler. As such, there were often some quite unpleasant evening meals at the Robbins house during the last few International seasons.

Ruben, who'd played with the Internationals the past year and was the team's leading scorer, was now heading back to Germany. He was an exchange student, and his time in the States had come to an end. The Internationals would never have won their first state championship without Ruben. This was a big loss for the team, both because of Ruben's talent and because he was so loved and respected by all his team-mates.

Ruben, our talented German striker

We'd also be losing JD, the young Wayne Rooney look-alike, who dropped out after the team returned from the summer tournament trip in Southern California.

I tried calling JD numerous times, but he was nowhere to be found. He'd struggled with alcohol and who knew what else? My heart went out to him as I knew he had a tough home life. JD had disappeared for short stints before, but I was usually able to find him and encourage him to come back, doing all I could to keep him on the team and out of trouble.

You can offer a hand, but if the other person doesn't reach out to grab that hand, there's not much else you can do.

Rumor had it that JD had run away. Like Erik, his friend and schoolmate, JD was a free spirit, a wild stallion, possibly never to be tamed.

He was a great player for the International, scored the goal in overtime that won the "Miracle Game at Camas," as well as many other assists and goals. He was the best I'd seen in his rare ability to earn PKs, with what came to be known as the "Duffy flop" for his last name—his uncanny ability to be brushed up against when going to goal and then take a dramatic dive or tumble, often leading to a PK call from the ref. I was grateful that JD had played as long as he had, but still felt bad I couldn't do anything to help him. More than anything, I wanted to help all of the boys grow up to become responsible adults, able to enjoy a good life.

I spent as much time and effort as I possibly could to help, especially those who didn't have fathers or positive male role models at home. Some I was able to help, others I couldn't, but as long as I was coaching, I wouldn't stop trying.

The team now joined the highest-level league we'd played in. Without Ruben and JD, we'd lost two of our top scorers. However, we still had Essa, Musie, Eamon, Tim, Riyen, Shivy, and several other talented offensive players and scorers; so, I wasn't expecting scoring to be a major problem, but it turned out that we ended up struggling for half the season, losing three games and tying two. Nevertheless, we still had managed enough wins to stay in the league championship hunt.

In one of the early games, Ethan, our goalkeeper, couldn't make the game, so Eric, the all-conference keeper who had joined us from Bill's team, took his place and when called to action, he definitely proved his worth. The other team got two penalty kicks, during the game and Eric made incredible saves on each of them. The Internationals pulled off a win that would never have happened had it not been for Eric's star performance.

The team kept the goals scored on us down, but we had a hard time scoring. We were getting shots, but the shots just weren't resulting in goals. I asked Danny Jackson, still our trainer, what we could do to score more?

Danny had worked on shooting with the guys, but this alone just wasn't getting the job done. He recommended we switch to a 4-3-3 formation. However, I was a bit nervous about doing this.

Although our team wasn't scoring many goals, we were still usually getting more shots than our opponents, so I wasn't sure why switching formations would help. If your team can't put the ball in the back of the net, no formation can change that.

The other concern was that while the 4-3-3 is a more offensive or attacking formation, it's also riskier defensively—a team is more susceptible to counterattacks with only three mid-fielders trying to cover a 70- or 80-yard-wide field. I'd coached this formation before for parts of games when the clock was winding down and the team needed to score, but it had never been our team's starting formation. Much of my coaching success to date had been due to my having a defensive mind-set.

I went along with Danny's suggestion, based on the fact that I realized we needed to make a change, believing in the adage that insanity is defined as doing the same thing over and over and expecting a different result. Maybe making this change was worth the risk defensively?

Midway through the season, Danny and I began training the team in the 4-3-3 formation. The first game we played in the new formation garnered six goals. I wasn't sure if we'd just discovered the Golden Fleece or if we happened to have played the league's weakest opponent.

The next game was a home game. Midway through, Stuart, now starting at outside back, collided with an opponent and went down, holding his knee and screaming in pain.

He was carried off the field and his mom took him to the ER. He had torn his MCL. Stuart hadn't been the easiest player to coach; he was talented, but I had struggled to get him to play the way I believed in playing.

Part of FC Shoreline International's success was that players understood our system of play and their role within the system. Along the way, a few players naturally may have initially challenged this, but they ultimately adapted to our team's style.

In Stuart's defense, he was fairly new to the team and hadn't had much time to make the adjustment to a new team and a new coach. He'd often make great offensive runs from his outside back position, but would then often casually jog back on defense, leaving the other three defenders to cover for him. This didn't make his fellow defenders very happy, nor me.

I'd yell at him to get back and kept urging him to think defense first, but Stuart always wanted to join the attack, which often placed extra pressure on the defense.

Now with a serious injury, his FC Shoreline International playing days were over. I checked on him several times after this injury, and thankfully, he made a full recovery a year later and went on to later play soccer at Evergreen State College.

The only possible silver lining to losing Aaron and Stuart was that subbing now became a little easier.

Whether it was the change to the 4-3-3 formation or because our long-time players finally established continuity with the new players as the season progressed, the Internationals didn't lose another game for the remainder of the season.

Unfortunately, because of the few losses early on, we finished 2nd in the league, which didn't really matter, because there was no longer promotion or relegation and we now, with the new state setup, were no longer allowed to play in the highest division. Still, this was the first time since we'd been a club team, that the Internationals hadn't finished in 1st place in our respective league.

The team went on to play in the President's Cup, the state tournament for teams at our level. We made it to the quarter-finals before being eliminated, not a bad result given the higher level of play, but nevertheless a disappointing finish to what had been our most challenging season yet.

Adding so many new players to the team and knowing most were one (season) and done, may have left some of our long-time players, as well as myself, feeling like something was missing that season. Maybe it could be compared to renting a car? It often takes a while to get used to driving a rental car and then as soon as you start to figure it out, it's time to return the car. There was just no feeling of permanence. The team didn't have the same family feeling we had in years past, and this likely showed on the pitch. Because soccer is the ultimate team game, continuity is king. Maybe adding all this new talent actually had a negative effect. Addition by subtraction, or is it subtraction by addition?

This is the beauty of the game: It's not the parts that make the machine...but rather how the parts all fit and function together that determines if the team can perform as a "well-oiled machine".

Soccer isn't like basketball, where one player can make a dominating impact, like a Michael Jordan, Kareem, Kobe, or Lebron. In baseball, an all-star pitcher like a Koufax or Kershaw can totally control the outcome of a game.

In football, one player can't make all the difference, but a team still usually needs a great QB like a Brady or Montana to win a championship. It's true that players like Ronaldo or Messi make a huge difference to their teams, but in the game of soccer, they can't win without a strong supporting cast. As great as Ronaldo is, Portugal never made it to the finals in the four times he played for his country in World Cup. This is certainly no slight on Ronaldo, only testament to the fact that one man, even one of the greatest to ever play the game, can't do it by himself.

In the game of futbol, it takes an entire team to succeed. The team must play together as one unit, to create a championship masterpiece.

* * *

Many of the boys were now heading off to college. Jacob, Bill's son, was moving on, as was Eric, the goalie from Bill's team. Charlie's cousin, Kue, and Nate from the Jetstream headed to college. Of the six players added to the team that past season, only Charley Newman remained.

Even Jamal was off to college, the boy, now a man, who six years earlier sat on the grass watching the Mad Dogs practice, the one who had told his ESL class about the team. The Internationals would never be the team they were if not for Jamal, an Ethiopian boy whose family fled their war-torn native country only to end up in a disease-ridden refugee camp in Kenya, then coming to a new country, speaking little or no English, with no real support system until he found this team.

From these difficult beginnings and incredible hardships, Jamal was now headed to Western Washington University on a full scholarship. This was no hand-out either. Jamal had earned his scholarship by staying up nights studying and earning almost straight A's in high school. I was incredibly proud of Jamal and what he had accomplished.

Jamal had a smile that lit up a room and a gentleness about him that won over everyone he met. I remembered taking Jamal to the local super-market where he applied for a part-time job. Jamal was nervous, as it was the first time he'd done anything like this, but I said, "Jamal, all you need to do is look your interviewer in the eye and flash that big beautiful smile of yours. If you do that, I guarantee you the job is yours."

Sure enough, he came out smiling as suggested, obviously having been given the job. Jamal would be greatly missed by his teammates and by me. Thankfully, younger brother Yaqub was still with the team. Some players were still in high school, and others were going to local community colleges but wanted to keep playing for the Internationals.

Tim, long-time Captain and back-bone of the team since the Mad Dog days, would be playing for Edmonds Community College in the fall during the International's regular season, but would join the team for state cup once his college season ended. As long as the players were under 19 years old by a certain time of the year, they were still eligible to play for our team.

CHAPTER 12

A NEW BLUE CREW

At the U-19 age level, there were only two divisions left. One division didn't start until late May, after the high school season ended. This division also included several teams east of the mountains—a four-hour drive. The second league played during the regular fall and early winter season and included only one team from a long distance away. It was an easy decision which league to play in.

It was great having many of the core International players back for their final season, but I quickly needed to find players to supplement the roster, especially a new goalie to replace Ethan, the affable German lad who'd been with our team for several years, as well as Eric, who'd only played with our team only that one season. I couldn't afford to wait until the tryouts to find a new goalie—keepers are a special bunch, and the good ones don't grow on trees.

I heard Lynnwood High School had a great goalie, seemingly an oxymoron since Lynnwood, at least in recent years, hadn't been known for their winning teams. If I looked at this as the glass being half full, maybe this meant their goalie had numerous opportunities to be tested. He was a big, strong, Uruguayan young man who, one game when coming out to get the ball, broke an attacking player's leg in the process. It was a fair play, but proved this goalie was big, strong, and tough. I attended a Lynnwood game to check him out. This could've been awkward because Jeremy, the one player I'd cut, still played for Lynnwood. I figured that if Jeremy still held a grudge, that was his problem. I also surmised, Jeremy being a starting defender for Lynnwood; it might also explain their team's struggles defensively. Though his team lost, the big Uruguayan goalie made some excellent saves that would have otherwise been sure goals. I was sold, not to mention we didn't have any other options at that point.

When the game ended, I walked up to him and introduced myself. "Hi, I'm Skip Robbins. I coach FC Shoreline International. You played a great game. What club team do you play for?"

The player, Emiliano, asked, "Club team?" and I said, "Yeah, don't you play for a club team when you're not playing for the school team?"

Emiliano shrugged. "No, those teams cost a lot."

I looked at the gloves Emiliano was wearing and said, "Those look pretty worn out."

"Yeah," Emiliano said, "but they still work."

"Our team has players from all over the world," I said. "How'd you like to play on our team? You won't have to pay a thing, and I'll even buy you new gloves. In fact, I think I have a pair in the car. What size do you wear?"

Emiliano, soon to be known as Emi, mumbled, "Uh, 11."

"Wait here...I'll get them."

I walked to my car, where I always carried extra soccer equipment. I handed Emi the new gloves, then went in for the close. "Enjoy 'em. Hey, can I get your number and I'll call you and we can get you signed up for our team? Our season doesn't start for a few more months, after your high school season is over."

Emi said, "Sounds good," and gave me his number. I kept in touch, came to another of Emi's games, and when his high school season had ended, Emi joined the International team.

I soon found out from Emi that his mother had passed away a few years earlier. He'd been living with his sister and her young son, his nephew. Emi's dad had a new girlfriend and his own place and there apparently wasn't room for Emi.

Emi's dad was Brazilian, but Emi, like his mother and sister, was born in Uruguay, in the capital city of Montevideo. He was about six years old when his family moved to the U.S. Emiliano Suarez proved to be an outstanding keeper for the International team, quite possibly the best we ever had.

* * *

Tryouts for the team were held in early June. The dates were listed on the FC Shoreline website. I wasn't sure how many players would show up. A few nights before the tryout date, I got a call from a woman doctor inquiring about the team. Doctor Hoock, or Jennifer as she asked to be called, found out about the Shoreline International tryouts on the internet. Could she bring Charlie to try out?

"Charlie doesn't speak much English. I met him in Guatemala where I spend a month every year providing free medical treatment for the indigent. He was living on the streets. His real name is Carlos, but I prefer Charlie, would hang around the medical clinic. The next year, when I returned to Guatemala, there was Charlie again, and that's when I invited him to the U.S. to stay with my family, feeling the experience could help him better his life."

I said, "Interesting...it doesn't really matter that he doesn't speak English. We have several boys on the team who speak Spanish and can help translate." I also explained that ours was a high-level club team. This wasn't rec soccer where every player makes the team.

"I understand," Jennifer said. "I got Charlie on a local rec team, but he didn't like it because none of the boys could even pass the ball accurately. This is why I'm calling you. I'm hoping to find a higher-level team for

Charlie to play on. I think he's a good player, but I can't swear to it...I don't know much about soccer."

"He's more than welcome to try out," I said, "but we only have a few roster spots open, so it won't be easy to make the team."

Another player I knew called a few nights before tryouts. Gerardo had played on another Evergreen team the Internationals faced in a friendly game a year back—a non-league game when two teams meet to help prepare for their league games.

I'd spoken to their coach, and we agreed to keep the game safe and under control, so no players got hurt before the big state tournament. The other team was largely Hispanic, and although a good team, was known to be aggressive.

The Internationals led by six goals with at least 30 minutes still to go. Peter was clearing the ball and, while doing so, Gerardo climbed on Peter's back and took him down to the ground. The ref red-carded Gerardo. Then another of his teammates intentionally and aggressively fouled another International, and he too was ejected. That was enough. I finally told the ref, who I'd hired for this "friendly" now turned unfriendly match, to call off the game to avoid any injuries. The ref whistled for the game to end. The other coach wasn't happy the game was called off, nor were some of their players, but the International team was so far ahead, it didn't matter anyway. Not to mention, the other team was now down two players because of their ejections, so I'm not sure why their coach was so eager for the game to continue? What I did know for sure was the only thing our Internationals had to lose at this point was risking one of our players being injured. Gerardo and I had a laugh over the phone about this incident, and I then welcomed him to come to the tryouts.

Another player emailed me about trying out. Jake Hibbard was referred to the team by Eamon. They both started for the same high school team, King's, a small local Christian school that was one of the top teams in the state at their level.

Tryout day came, and we ended up having a large turnout, about 20 players, many more than I had expected. Maybe this was a sign that the International team's reputation had spread.

Our long-time International players remembered Gerardo, and a few approached me to express their concerns about him. My response was to give him a chance. Most the players weren't up to snuff, but a few were excellent. Charlie, the young man from Guatemala turned out to be a very pleasant surprise. He was even smaller than Musie, but his ball control was incredible. He could dribble at full speed and, when doing so, the ball looked like it was glued to his feet. He also had a great cross, as well as a wicked shot. Charlie was clearly going to be a major impact player. He couldn't speak a lick of English, but Gerardo and Emi helped translate.

The "three amigos," strangers till that tryout day, bonded right then and there. This was huge for little Charlie. Gerardo and Emi made him feel comfortable and helped translate any necessary communication. I later found out more of Charlie's story from Jennifer. He had come from a large and very poor family. His mother was an alcoholic. She died when Charlie was only eight years old, and he never knew his father. They lived in poverty in Guatemala City. After his mom's death, Charlie and the siblings went to live with the oldest brother. However, he left Charlie and a younger brother to live alone in a shed without any water, toilet, or electricity.

They were left to beg on the streets for money and food. During this time, Charlie developed appendicitis and had to take the bus by himself to the hospital to have emergency surgery.

Later, around the time he was 12 years old, he and his brother Cuzy went to live with the next older brother. They all lived in the attic in their godmother's house. At 16, Charlie dropped out of school and left for the streets.

He survived by running errands for a local gang. Fortunately, he never joined the gang. Although not educated, he still had a strong conscience and knew what he had been doing was wrong.

He had nowhere else to go, so he finally went to a local church to try to turn his life around. The church worked with local youth, many of whom had been in gangs. They had a food program and more. In 2008, the founder of the church offered Charlie the opportunity to travel with a medical team that was visiting from Seattle in 2008. This was where Charlie met Dr. Jennifer and her partner, Sean. After bonding with the affable Charlie, Jennifer and Sean decided to invite Charlie to live with their family in the U.S.

They knew very little about Charlie, not even realizing he was 18 years old, thinking he was several years younger. After many months of trying to make arrangements, Charlie was finally given a Student Visa through Kaplan to study English. He arrived in Seattle in 2009, just a few months before the team tryouts. Charlie had never before lived in a real house or had a refrigerator filled with food that he could eat whenever he wanted. He had never had people who cared about him, where he was, or how he was doing. Because of some things he'd done in his past, he felt he was a bad person, who didn't deserve all that was happening to him. He was grateful, but also very confused. Since Jennifer and her family spoke limited Spanish and Charlie could speak very little English, communication was challenging.

However, Jennifer did learn that Charlie loved soccer and had some skills, though she didn't know much about the game herself, nor did Sean. Their 16-year-old son played on a local rec team. Charlie practiced with the team and though it soon became clear that he had never played organized soccer before; it was also clear he was far more skilled than any of the players on this low-level team. However, he still had no idea about positioning or the intricacies of the game, other than what he had seen a few times at local games or on television in the rec room at the church.

Moreover, Jennifer saw how much Charlie loved playing soccer and it was obvious that he needed to play at a much higher level than rec. She asked around and somehow discovered that there was a high-level team, named FC Shoreline International, which would soon be holding tryouts. She called me up one evening and said our team sounded like the perfect team for Charlie. However, after hearing that Charlie had no organized soccer experience, I tried to let her down easy, cautioning that it wouldn't be easy for Charlie to make our team, not wanting her or Charlie to be disappointed. On tryout day, she spoke to several of the moms there and found out even more about the skill and talent of the boys on this team. Knowing so little about soccer, she had no idea if Charlie would be talented enough to make this team.

It didn't take long to see that he most definitely did have the talent and would be a great addition to our team.

Gerardo also looked sharp at the tryouts. We could see he could be a big help to the team playing either striker or center mid. He'd been named to the all-conference team when he played for Cascade High School in Everett.

He couldn't afford to pay much, but I offered to pay his fees in exchange for Gerardo agreeing to drive Emi to and from practices and games, an arrangement that worked out well for all three of us.

Jennifer and her family thankfully could afford to pay Charlie's club fees. I never made a player decision based on money. I was fine with paying for a player if he was a good addition to the team. I rarely recruited players, though I always had my eyes and ears open. In spite of the ample talent on the International team, I could've recruited better players, but that was not what the International team was about.

We found players through tryouts or when a player showed up out of nowhere or on those rare occasions when I heard about a talented player, such I had with Ruben earlier on and Emi more recently.

We kept finding new players in a myriad of ways. Most club teams wouldn't hesitate to cut a player who'd been with the team for years, if a better player came along and they were forced to make the choice. I never cut players who'd been on the team for a long time and who fit in.

The International team was more like a family. It might be different if the player was only with our team for a short time, but fortunately, things always seemed to work out and I only had to cut a few players over my many years coaching our team.

There were one or two, including Jeremy, that I had to cut, and several others that I cut after a few practices, when it became apparent, they weren't up to snuff. This only happened a few times in the five years the International team had been in existence. One of these was a young man from Thailand, who'd been trying out even though he had a severely sprained ankle. His name was incredibly long and difficult to pronounce. The evaluators and I couldn't get a fair read on his skills, because his ankle was injured. However, we were all impressed with his grit and perseverance, so we invited him to practice with the team when his ankle had healed, and if he looked good, we told him he'd get a spot. Once he was back to form, it became clear that he was too raw to play at the level required. We liked him, but at U-19, there just wasn't enough time to bring him up to snuff.

Every so often, a new player showed up that fit the team like a glove. Charley Newman had been this kind of player and, as the team soon discovered, so was Jake Hibbard, Eamon's high school teammate. Jake would prove to be an instrumental player for the Internationals.

It wasn't very long before he was voted a captain by the players. Jake had played for quite a few other clubs and teams, and he was impressed by how all of the players welcomed him right away. He later told me that he'd never been on a team where there were no huge egos and everyone seemed to have their roles. He felt "it was truly a brotherhood and that there just seemed to be a certain unspoken bond on the Internationals that he hadn't experienced before. Everyone just seemed to gel." He went on to say, "It was a true meshing of different backgrounds, races, religions...everyone I'm sure had their personal beliefs, but it didn't matter to any of us because we all shared one common bond—we all loved to play soccer. At the end of the day, we just had fun together and played for each other. Man, I just loved it."

I thought Jake's words captured the essence of our team, probably better than even I could have expressed it.

One of the additional bonuses at tryouts was that Jake's dad, Randy Hibbard, agreed to join us as an assistant coach. Randy had played in college, coached college soccer, and later club soccer. Randy turned out to be a great guy and he and I soon became good friends. The players also quickly took to Randy and listened with open ears and respect, whenever he had something to say.

The tryouts over, Little Charlie (nickname to distinguish him from Charley Newman), Gerardo, and Jake were absolute no-brainers to make the team. A few others were on the cusp.

One of these was Ben, a player from a small Christian school in Shore-line. Ben, who'd already graduated, said their high school team wasn't very good and that he, not to brag, was the best player at his school. He was fast, had a big boot, and good skills. He looked to be a strong role player, though probably not a starter, so he was given a spot on the team.

The last player we added was Milen, born in Bulgaria, who'd been a starting defender for nearby Edmonds High School. I doubted Milen would crack our starting lineup or earn a lot of playing time, but we decided to add him because we needed more depth on defense.

I didn't like to sub much on the back line and didn't usually need to, with Peter, Yaqub, Pemba, and big Charley back there. These guys were all lock-down defenders. Peter was attending the University of Washington, but lived close enough to make most practices and games.

I had always said when Peter was done playing for the team, it was time for me to retire. That's how good Peter was. Tim, our long-time co-captain from England, along with Peter, both with us since the Mad Dogs years, now played for Edmonds Community College. He'd be able to join the team for state cup after the regular season ended, but his college season was at the same time as the International season, so he wouldn't be able to make any practices or games, until his college season was over. Charley Newman and Jake would soon be named captains along with our team's perennial captain, Peter.

The team still had a strong International flavor with Peter (Japan), Tim (England), Pemba (Nepal), Essa (Gambia), Riyen (Holland/Lebanon), Musie (Eritrea), Yaqub (Ethiopia), Shivy (Fiji), and Emiliano aka Emi (Uruguay/Brazil). Now we added little Charlie (Guatemala), Gerardo (Mexico), and Milen (Bulgaria). Regardless of how many or few international players there were, there was never any intention of becoming more international or purposely adding International players. That all just happened. Nevertheless, having players from so many countries sure made our team banquets more interesting, more fun and a lot tastier too.

* * *

Charlie Morales aka "Little Charlie"

Jake Hibbard

Emiliano "Emi" Suarez

Charley Newman

Gerardo Martinez-Alfaro

CHAPTER 13

SWAN SONG SUMMER

The team began practicing in late June. Our very first game was a friendly match vs. Shoreline Community College—an important early test playing against a college team. The teams proved to be fairly well matched, and the game ended in a 2–2 draw. The Shoreline coach, though disappointed his team was tied by a club team, was glad his team was tested and asked if we could schedule another game soon.

We next entered a tournament up north, in Skagit. The International team had trouble scoring in this tournament. We gave up very few goals, but still lost two of our four games because we just weren't scoring much. We ended up not making the semi's—definitely not the norm for this team.

However, I wasn't overly concerned. When a team had new players, I knew it took time for everyone to become familiar with one another.

I had to figure out the players' best positions, their style of play, and train the new players on what was expected of them. These things take time, which was one of the reasons I entered our team in so many summer tournaments. These games allowed our team time to work out the kinks before the regular season began.

I learned something new at the Skagit Tournament. Turned out the team had a ritual that every new player on the team had to endure. I found out about this when we went out to lunch between games. I guessed that either Essa or Tyler were likely the originators of this ritual.

The boys, while at lunch or dinner, would fill a tall glass with every possible ingredient they could find, and the new player would have to drink at least a few gulps.

These revolting concoctions would often include mustard, ketchup, sugar, salt, pepper, butter, red pepper flakes, chocolate shake, ground-up hamburger, salad dressing, sodas, lemonade, pizza cheese—anything at all they found at the table or could get their hands on. The ingredients would then be stirred until liquified and served to the new player.

The only reason I found out about this was because while the players were at lunch at a local Red Robin, the concoction was served to Ben who, after drinking it, heaved all over the table. I joined the laughs, then made the boys clean up the disgusting mess.

The next tournament was the Starfire Tournament. Starfire was a huge soccer complex with eight full turf fields and a beautiful stadium out in Tukwila, where we'd won our first state championship. Our team's first game was against a pretty good team, and I was confident the Internationals would take them, but once again, we struggled to score and the game ended in a scoreless tie. I was now starting to be concerned. We had too much firepower not to be scoring goals. With attackers like Essa, Musie, Gerardo, Eamon, little Charlie, Riyen and Shivy, this didn't make sense.

Our defense was looking great! Charley Newman and Peter as our center backs with Yaqub occasionally stepping into that position, plus Pemba and Yaqub as our starting outside backs. Jake Hibbard was doing an outstanding job as our defensive mid, and Emi was our superstar goalkeeper. The D was definitely solid. However, a team still needed to score goals in order to consistently win games.

The next game was later that day. I decided to change things up. We'd be playing an aggressive and talented Hispanic team. I assembled the troops on a vacant field at the Starfire complex and shared the new plan—a sure-fire guaranteed win, but only if every player followed the plan.

I called it "60 Minutes from Hell" for the opposing team if the International players followed the plan through to the "T."

I'd briefly scouted the team we were about to play and noticed they liked to pass the ball in their defensive third and try to frustrate and wear out the opposing team's attackers by getting them to chase after the ball. My plan was to apply a high-pressure defense that would allow our guys to win balls in the opposition's defensive third, our attacking third. I had the offensive players in their usual formation, then put the defenders back there. We would attack if the ball went to their right back. Whoever played the left mid would arc his run and trap that player in the corner. The left back for the Internationals now had to move up to mark their right mid. The International striker (Essa or Gerardo) would have to mark their closest center back. The center mid, Eamon, would mark their center mid, and our defensive center mid, Jake, would mark their other center mid, and so on. Almost every player on the opposing team would need to be tightly marked. If the guys did this properly, they'd win balls in front of the other team's goal and thereby create excellent scoring opportunities.

It was high pressure with tight man marking, not exactly re-inventing the wheel, but nevertheless effective, if played as designed. We reviewed and practiced this in shadow play for about 30 minutes, then left to warm up for the game.

The Internationals came out breathing fire, playing with great energy and emotion. Our defense was smothering and, with our quickness and athleticism, the guys followed through with the plan and it worked like a charm. We scored three goals in the first half and two more in the second. Our opponent was thoroughly frazzled. The Internationals were now a new and improved team. I got all the guys pizza at the restaurant on the second level at Starfire, and we then headed home to rest up and get ready to return for tomorrow's game.

Before leaving Starfire, I went over to look at the tournament board to find out who we would be playing next game and at what time and field.

It turned out we were going to play Crossfire's top team. Crossfire was a big club east of Lake Washington, considered the elite club in the state. They also represented everything I felt was wrong about club soccer, which was a lot. In spite of coaching club, I wasn't a fan of the club system. It was a fixed game. I felt the state should run the leagues strictly on the basis of promotion and relegation, similar to the Premiership in England and other top leagues around the world. You finish in the top two or three in your league and you move up; you finish in the bottom two or three, you move down. No elite club should be able to play in a league that denies play for another club. I especially didn't like the fact that youth soccer in America was becoming a rich kid's sport.

The kids from lower economic homes couldn't afford to play club soccer, and if you don't play club soccer, you often don't make the high school team, and if you don't make the high school team, you sure can't play soccer in college, and if you can't play soccer in college, no way can you play professionally. The club system, although offering a few scholarships, was like a fancy country club where only the elite can join.

I believed this was one of the main reasons the USA men's team hadn't fared well in international competitions. The vast majority of the top athletes in the U.S. were playing basketball, football, and baseball. Most kids were being denied the opportunity to play soccer at a competitive level. Even if a few scholarships were given, how do kids in the inner city or from poorer communities even find out about a scholarship?

The exception might be women's soccer. Soccer is more popular among girls in the U.S. than it is in many other countries, where religions and cultures often don't allow or encourage girls to play sports. This was one of a myriad of reasons why the U.S.A. Women's team was usually the best or among the best in the world.

Some made the argument that the USA wasn't faring as well in men's soccer because there are so many other sports to compete with in the U.S. This is true, but how does that explain the USA with over 325 million people losing to Trinidad and Tobago with a population of 1.4 million, or losing to Costa Rica with a population of 5 million, and how about when a small country like Iceland, population 340,000, can qualify and do well in the last World Cup? Croatia made the finals in the 2018 World Cup with a population of only 4 million people. I call out the "pay to play" club system in our country, where player club fees usually range from $2,000 to $5,000 and up. How many families can afford to pay this kind of money for their child to play soccer?

I've also heard or read that many of the soccer coaches and author-ities of the game feel that the USA men's team players seem to lack creativity in the final third and as a result also don't have the same ability to finish, i.e., score goals as do many of the more international players. Could this be because of the "one size fits all" formal training that the young American born players receive? How else could one explain our team's success. Half or more of our players never had any formal soccer training until they came to the U.S. Yet, so many of them like Jamal, Yaqub, Pemba, Riyen, Shivy, Essa, Musie, little Charlie had better ball control than most American players who had the benefit of high-level formal training since they were six or seven years old. Most or at least a significant number of our players learned to play futbol on the streets or in dirt fields and didn't even have real soccer balls to play with when growing up. This lack of formal training at this young age might be more similar to how many of the world's best players learned to play the game. Did these kids from other parts of the world learn creativity and ball control all on their own, without a coach telling or teaching them how to control the ball?

I certainly couldn't say, but I did find this at least curious? I was confident that I had little to do with teaching our players the moves that they seemed to innately possess.

These club teams certainly required coaches with formal training. The licensing for coaches in the U.S. required attending courses that I found to be quite restrictive, almost as if there was only one way to coach.

How was it that my teams quite often beat teams with A and B licensed coaches? I only had a National D license, which was probably as far as I could go since I hadn't ever played the game at a high level. You could be a soccer genius, but if you didn't play in college or professionally, your chances were very slim in obtaining an A or B or possibly even a C license.

These licensing courses required the coaches to participate and it became quite clear that if you weren't a very good player, they didn't want you to pass the course. This may be denied by some of the soccer powers-to-be, but most coaches will tell you this is true.

Nevertheless, not having the highest-level coaching license never bothered me, not even the slightest. After coaching for so many years, I had the experience and the resume to coach for just about any club I wanted to and be paid to do so. However, I refused to be paid.

FC Shoreline had a few paid coaches, and there were pressures in the works to eliminate volunteer coaches like me. I knew that having only paid coaches would just result in higher club fees for the players and I wanted any player to be able to play soccer at the club level, regardless of their family's financial status.

Instead of being paid, I was doing the paying, spending upwards of $30,000 a year to help the boys from lower-economic families play soccer.

I also felt a responsibility as a coach to teach the players more than just soccer, to help the boys grow up to become successful adults, teaching them about responsibility, timeliness, courtesy, empathy, developing a work ethic, learning to work as a team, learning how to control emotions and many other important life skills that would hopefully serve them well their entire lives.

I believe there has to be a way to encourage and allow the incredible young athletes who grow up to play professional basketball, baseball, and football in packed arenas and crowded stadiums across our country, to have the same opportunity to play soccer, if they so choose. It's the world's most popular sport, yet because of the club system, the doors in our country are shut for most kids from lower economic homes, resulting in what I believe is financial bias and economic discrimination. To some degree, a case could even be made for racial discrimination.

I was excited we'd have the chance to play against an elite team like Crossfire. We'd never have the opportunity to play them in league or even post-season play because our International team was no longer allowed to compete in their exclusive league.

I spent that evening before our game preparing the game plan and my pre-game talk.

I normally wasn't one to give motivational speeches before a game, mostly instructional and strategic advice and maybe a short pep talk, like, "Okay, let's go, 100% effort 100% of the game," or just a sentence or two to try to pump them up or maybe a quote to inspire them.

I'm not a big believer in getting players too hyped up. As mentioned earlier, my all-time favorite coach in any sport is John Wooden, the Hall of Fame UCLA basketball coach. Wooden believed that if players get too up, they're likely to get too down as well.

He didn't want his players to play emotionally, because emotion could adversely affect their judgment.

Wooden believed the game was won at practices, which was why he'd sit on the bench during games, holding a program rolled up in his hands, looking as calm and collected, as if he was at the library or a classroom. Wooden felt his job was pretty much done at game time. It was up to the players to execute what they'd practiced.

I could never be that calm. I was more the emotional, passionate type who tried his best to stay calm.

Sometimes I achieved this, and sometimes my temperamental nature got the better of me. I agreed that pumping players up usually lasted only a few minutes, if that. I also agreed with Wooden's philosophy that games are won at practices. Wooden's UCLA teams, fundamentally sound, often looked like they were putting on a clinic when out on the hardwood.

This game, however, was one of those games that called for an inspirational speech, maybe because of my feelings about elite clubs like Crossfire.

One thing I knew for sure, we couldn't use the same strategy from our last game; it wouldn't work against this team. We had to play our regular style and rise to the occasion. I hoped that last game would give our team the confidence they needed. If you believe you can do something, you often can.

Conversely, if you don't believe you can, you're usually right as well. Much of the success in soccer and other sports is what's between the players' ears, as well as in their hearts.

"I want you to take a look at the other team," I said. "This is *the* elite club, one of the most prestigious clubs in the state. Very few of you can afford the fees to play for Crossfire. A lot of you might not even be able to afford the boots these guys are wearing. These guys have every advantage you don't have. They're all from wealthy families, live in mansions, drive expensive cars, they'll go to the top colleges and their daddies will pay their way. The doors that are wide open to these players are closed shut to you. Today, in this game, you have an opportunity—the chance to prove that you don't have to be rich to be a great soccer player, you don't have to have a lot of money to have courage, to have heart, to have the will to win. You have the opportunity today, in this game, to show them what you can do. You may not have the same privileges, you may never have the same opportunities, but today, in this game, this is your opportunity.

Let's show them who we are—a team made up of players from many countries, religions, and races, all of whom have love for one another, who've come together as a band of brothers. Let's do battle as brothers and show these guys what unity and brotherhood can accomplish. Make them remember this day, the day they played FC Shoreline International."

FC Shoreline controlled the game from the opening kick-off to the final whistle. Our guys played with intensity and fire the entire game. Crossfire ended up scoring one goal. FC Shoreline International scored four in a game they would never forget—the underdog team from the club no one had heard of beat the all-mighty Crossfire.

One play in particular memorialized this game for every player, every coach, every fan who was there that day.

Little Charlie, with his back to the goal, received the ball and executed a highlight film, a picture-perfect bicycle kick sending an unstoppable shot into the upper V—one of the greatest goals anyone watching that game or any game had ever seen or would see. Little Charlie, from the streets of Guatemala, lit up like a Christmas tree, as did all of our International players, as well as every parent, coach, and fan. The players embraced one another in one giant group hug, and the boys all lifted Charlie up in the air. Charlie had been initiated in this game, forever earning the love and respect of his teammates.

Charlie's bicycle kick vs Crossfire

Celebrating Little Charlie's amazing goal

We qualified for the tournament championship to be played the next day in Starfire Stadium, the very same stadium where the Internationals almost two years earlier had won our first state championship.

Sunday afternoon, the guys returned to play FC Alliance Gold, which had won the state championship the previous year. This game didn't go quite as well. No fairy tale endings this time around.

Alliance sent impressively long and accurate switches and uncharacteristically caught our defense out of position. A switch is a ball passed or kicked from one side of the field to the opposite side in order to catch the opposing defense out of position. In soccer, defenses are usually taught to compact the opposing offense, so when the attacking team is at one side of the field, the defense will usually try to have their players on that side, shutting down space and narrowing the passing lanes, so the opposing offense has difficulty connecting their passes.

The International defense was doing a fine job, compacting their offense to one side, however the Alliance took advantage of this by keeping an attacking player wide and sending long and accurate switches to that player, who in turn controlled the ball with one touch and headed for goal.

The Alliance scored twice on these long switches. The International attackers had our chances, but couldn't score. We lost the championship game 0–2. We had lost to the better team this game, but still had a great tournament. We'd take this experience and build on it and keep making progress, as the summer wore on.

* * *

When I arranged the summer tournaments, I wanted to find one tournament we were almost sure to win, another tournament or two where we had a chance to win, but it wouldn't be easy, and a tournament that would be a reach for the team, playing superior teams very difficult to compete against. As most coaches agree, playing better competition makes you better, forces you to rise up and improve your game.

It was difficult to gauge how good our FC Shoreline International team really was. The team had started four years ago, at the lowest division in club soccer. We'd won our league championship almost every year and continued to move up the ladder, to increaslingly stronger divisions. In only one season had the Internationals not won their league, when we finished in 2nd place at the highest level we'd played at. Had I not added so many new players, I believe we would've won that league as well. The question remained: how good were we? We wouldn't be allowed to play at the highest level, now closed to all but the largest and most elite clubs in the state.

I wanted the team to be tested, so I called the tournament director for one of the most prestigious tournaments in the state, the Pacific Coast Invitational Tournament, held up in Bellingham, Washington.

Teams had to be invited to play in this prestigious tournament, and normally a team from a club like FC Shoreline wouldn't be included. FC Shoreline was a neighborhood club, looked down upon by the bigger, more prestigious clubs, if they'd even heard of FC Shoreline. Luck had it that they had an opening to fill for a team in their combined U-18/U-19 age group.

I'd been honored as the Coach of the Year for the State of Washington in 2008, the previous year, and the tournament director knew of me because he'd been on the panel of judges.

I'd been awarded this honor, not necessarily because of the International team's success on the soccer field, but because the state officials had heard about our unique team and how I had helped out so many boys from other countries.

Sue Brangwin, a wonderful woman who'd selflessly served on the Hillwood Soccer Board for many years dating back to the Mad Dog years, had unbeknownst to me, nominated me for Coach of the Year for the Seattle Youth Soccer Association and that had been the catalyst for the powers-that-be in the state learning about our unique team and how they discovered my efforts in helping many of the immigrant players on our team.

The tournament was a month away, and I started having second thoughts. Had I entered the team in a tournament in which we didn't belong? This tournament featured the top teams in the entire state. We'd played some really good teams before, but every team in this tournament was a high-level premier team.

Had I set the guys up for disaster? I wasn't sure, but just to "test the waters", I called a coach of another high-level team at the same age group and asked if he was interested in taking our spot in the tournament. He responded they'd already committed to another tournament out of state.

I soon realized the worst that could happen was that we would get hammered. That happened down at the San Diego Tournament the year before, and it hadn't been catastrophic, so I decided to stay the course. Once resolved, I looked for a hotel near the fields where the team could stay while playing in the tournament.

Sherri heard about a Water Ski Ranch in Bow Lake that was within a 30-minute drive of the soccer fields. She thought that might be fun for the boys.

The "Ranch" was owned by the same family that owned the famous northwest hamburger chain, Dick's Drive-In, the well-regarded Spady family. I called the ranch way ahead of time and was able to reserve the entire complex for the tournament dates.

The team arrived at the Water Ski Ranch a day before the tournament started, and the guys spent the day water skiing, playing basketball in the full court gym, and enjoying a myriad of other activities. In addition to the boys having fun when they stayed at places like this, it also helped the guys new to the team get to know their teammates better within a short amount of time. That evening at dinner, I gave a brief talk about tomorrow's tournament.

I let the team know they would be playing some of the best teams in the state, but I felt they were up to the task. I went on to say that history has proven that on any given day, any team can beat another.

That's the nature of sports. I gave the examples of the U.S.A. defeating England in the 1950 World Cup, the U.S.A. hockey team upsetting the Russians in the 1980 Olympics and the NY Jets beating the Colts in Superbowl III. These were just a few examples; there were thousands more upsets in sports history. Then I relayed to them the story of Roger Bannister and the four-minute mile. How before the 1950's, many scientists believed that the human body wasn't physically capable of running any faster than a four-minute mile. After thousands of years, no one had ever run the mile in under four minutes. Then on May 6th, 1954, Roger Bannister ran a 3:59 mile. He was a medical student at Oxford at the time and as part of his training, he relentlessly visualized breaking the four-minute mile in order to create a sense of certainty in his mind and body. Once he had accomplished this historic feat, another runner soon after broke this barrier as well and soon, quite a few runners were running the mile in under four minutes. Now a days, I told them, even many top high school runners can run the mile in less than four minutes. This just proves that if we work hard and we believe something, it can have a huge influence on the results. Our minds often make the difference between success and failure. If you think you can or you think you can't, either way, you're probably going to prove yourself right.

The next day, after a nice breakfast and a brief rest, the team headed to the fields. The first game was against the host team, the Whatcom Rangers—a highly ranked team that played in the highest league, PDL 1. The Internationals started out with a bang, scoring twice in the first half. It looked like we could not only play with these teams, maybe we could even shine against them.

The second half began, and the two teams battled, but the Internationals controlled the ball and looked to be the superior team. I was, however, concerned about the Ranger's right mid, he looked to be fast, elusive, and dangerous. I later found out that I had been right to be worried about him, as he was a former Academy player who happened to be guest playing for this team. Academy teams are the top teams in the State, even above P1 and compete against other Academy teams, mostly from other states

We were missing Peter for this tournament. He was working on a commercial fishing boat up in Alaska. Peter was definitely our best defender, possibly even the best player on the International team ever since he first started playing for the Mad Dogs, back in 2001.

Missing Peter and knowing that Milen, though a decent backup, wasn't the equal of most of our International defenders, I invited a guest player that Charley Newman recommended to join us for the tournament. Jeff was a school teammate of Charley's.

They both played for Bishop Blanchet, a Catholic school in Seattle. Guest players were allowed in non-season tournaments as long as they had a state player card, which Jeff did.

Jeff was playing left back in this tournament, and I was nervous, not because Jeff wasn't an excellent defender, but because on his side of the field, he was going up against the same skilled right mid that I'd been so concerned about. About halfway through the second half, that same attacker got the ball on the right flank, was able to get past Jeff, and fired a hard and perfectly aimed shot into the near post and into the back of the net. The Rangers were now down only one goal. Ten minutes later, that same attacker created enough space to send a long line-drive rocket into the upper v of the far post, an amazing shot that Emi had no chance to save. The game was tied. I thought about switching Pemba, the outside back on the opposite side with Jeff, but that would've been a slap in the face to the guest player and I recognized that even Pemba might struggle against this particular attacker.

I asked Jake Hibbard, playing defensive mid, to pay special attention to the player who'd scored the two goals. With 10 minutes to go, another one of the Ranger attackers dribbled into the 18-yard box. Charley, playing center back, stepped up to defend when the attacker flopped to the ground, pretending he was tripped.

Charley hadn't been close enough to trip him and couldn't believe the ref blew the whistle and gave the Rangers an undeserved PK. None of the International players could figure it out, nor could I. They loudly protested to the ref, but their lament fell on deaf ears.

This seemed like it had to be "a homer call"—a local ref trying to ensure the home team wins. In the hundreds of games I'd coached, I faced only a few situations where the ref was intentionally making calls against my team. More often, it was just incompetence, poor judgement, or faulty eyesight.

There wasn't a soccer coach alive, nor would there ever be, who couldn't come up with a lengthy list of horrendous calls made against their team over the course of their career. I certainly had such a list.

In fact, possibly for my own sanity as a coach, I invoked my own "Ref Therapy" and occasionally shared my creative concept with some of my fellow coaches. I created an imaginary game show. In this mythical show, a posse of coaches would assemble a group of the most incompetent refs we'd ever experienced and load them all into the back of a big truck, then we'd drive to a remote spot in the wilderness.

The coaches would all be armed with paint guns. We'd then release these regrettable refs into the woods and give them a five-minute head start. Then we'd hunt them down and pay them back for all the bad calls they'd made. Obviously, this was purely imaginary, meant entirely as a joke, but every coach I shared my game show idea with, absolutely loved the concept.

The PK taker, the same talented player who already scored the two earlier goals, took the PK and fired a perfectly placed ground ball inside the left post. He now had a hat-trick, and the Rangers were up by a goal. The Internationals desperately tried to equalize in the short time left, attacking furiously, but no cigar. The whistle blew to end the game. Our guys were naturally very upset, all of us feeling we were robbed, but we were also now fully confident that we could play with these elite teams.

One thing I'd noticed from the past games and tournaments was that Little Charlie needed more space to operate. Playing in the crowded middle and being short and light in weight, he was getting bumped and banged where gravity often won those battles. The bigger defenders knocked him around. I decided to push Little Charlie out to left mid for this next game, where he'd have more space to operate.

Playing the number two team in the state didn't faze the Internationals one bit. The guys were confident from the start and highly effective as well. Moving Little Charlie out to left mid turned out to be the right decision.

He was now tearing up the competition, beating one defender after another, showing his incredible skill and realizing his potential, as I knew he would.

The team looked fantastic playing a 4-4-2 with Essa and Gerardo up top, four mids, Charlie on the left (with Shivy subbing), Jake and Eamon, the King's duo at center mids (with Jamal subbing in), and Riyen out wide right (with Ben and Tyler subbing). The back line was Yaqub and Big Charley at center mid, Jeff at left back and Pemba on the right, with Milen subbing in when needed.

At goalkeeper was Emi, whom I affectionally called "The Big Easy," because he was big and made everything he did look easy. He moved slowly when not in the net, but still with a certain grace.

This didn't stop him from being a great goalie, possibly the best I'd coached. The Internationals, in just a 60-minute game (versus 90 minutes for league play and state cup), won 5–0, thrashing the number two team in Washington State.

After that game, the Emerald City Coach, one of the elite clubs in the state at that time, along with Crossfire, asked me what club we were with.

"We're FC Shoreline International," I replied.

He then asked, "Your team has so many players from…" Pausing, puzzled, I could see he was looking for the right words. "Uh, different backgrounds?"

I answered him, "Yeah, we have players from about 14 or 15 different countries, just about every race and religion, but they're all brothers on the pitch. We all wear blue." Then, not being able to pass up the opportunity, I said, "I just wish every club would give boys like ours the opportunity to afford to play club soccer and to be allowed to play in the top leagues."

We chatted for a while longer, and he responded kindly by agreeing that was indeed a problem with youth soccer in our country.

The next day, we beat the number five team in the state 3–0. Our goal differential was by far the best in the entire field of 16 teams. This was the good news.

The not-so-good news was there were four brackets with four teams in each bracket and only one winner came out of each bracket.

Since International was in the same bracket as the Rangers team that had beat us in that first game, and since the Rangers didn't lose a game in their bracket, though their games were much closer, they went on, and our FC Shoreline International team went home, but not before we had time to enjoy the Ski Ranch. The Pacific Coast Invitational proved that the Internationals were now one of the top teams in the State of Washington.

* * *

The 2009 season brought more changes. The Seattle Sounders were added to the top professional league in the U.S., the MLS (Major League Soccer). Previous to this, they played in the USL, the second division professional league. The Sounders hired a new coach, Sigi Schmid, a well-known and highly regarded German-American and former UCLA player and coach who'd already won several MLS championships.

Brian Schmetzer, who I had always been impressed with when he coached the USL Sounders, was named assistant coach.

Danny Jackson, who trained the International team for the past few years and was the Sounders team captain and All-Star center back as well as having been named the league's Defender of the Year, turned out to be the last player cut from the new MLS Sounders team. Danny was upset, not ready to end his soccer career, was only 30, and had at least several good years left. To add insult to injury, Sigi Schmid gave Danny the bad news in a hotel bar, only several feet away from his teammates.

I found out about this because Danny and I had become close over the years. Danny invited me to some Sounders get-togethers, and Sherri and I were guests at Danny's and his beautiful bride, Brianne's, wedding the previous year. Danny was a total gentleman, soft-spoken, smart, thoughtful, and kind, as well as a great trainer and friend. The boys on the team all loved and respected Danny.

Now with a wife to support and soon a family, Danny didn't want to play for another team and have to move to a new city.

He felt it was time to find a full-time job in the business world. I must confess; though I continued to support the Sounders, I never forgave Sigi for treating my friend and our wonderful trainer in such a disrespectful manner.

The team needed a new trainer and we had just the man, Toby Rawlinson, our team's goalkeeper trainer the past two years.

In his younger days, Toby played professionally in England and later served as a strategic analyst for Arsenal, the famous EPL club.

He was a good guy and proved to be another great trainer, though with his extremely strong English accent, the players and I would occasionally need Toby to translate, or rather explain what he'd just said in an accent we could understand!

CHAPTER 14

TRIALS AND TRIBULATIONS

The league the Internationals were now in was different from any other league we'd been in before. In most leagues, the competition was usually fairly equal from top to bottom. While one team might win every one of their games and another team might lose every game, the games were normally not runaways. This was because the teams had earned their way into that league, based on their record from the previous season. There were, of course, major exceptions to this rule, but there was usually a reason for any exception: maybe a team had lost several top players from the previous year or they had players injured or they'd picked up great players and were therefore much improved from the previous year. Most leagues had some degree of parity, but at the U-19 age level, leagues weren't always like that because there were only two leagues available and, thus, the quality of teams in these leagues could run the gamut.

The International's new league had three quality teams at the top, including the Internationals, another five so-so teams in the middle of the pack, and two extremely weak teams, more along the level of rec teams. With our International team being so strong now, I didn't expect we'd be tested often. We had Essa and Gerardo as strikers, Charlie at left mid, Musie, Eamon, and Jake rotating at center mid, Riyen and Ben alternating at right mid, and the back-line was Yaqub at left back, Pemba at right back, and Peter and "Big" Charley at center back with Emi as our keeper, Shivy subbing in at left mid, Tyler subbing in at right mid, and Milen getting minutes subbing in at a defender spot. This was, no doubt, a talented squad.

The Internationals won our first game 5–1. Our second game was against one of the worst teams we'd ever played, and we embarrassingly won 17–0. We tried to keep the score down, subbing players constantly. We moved our defensive players up to offense and offensive players to defense, wanting to allow everyone an opportunity to score. Every player on the team ended up scoring a goal. Even Emi, the goalie, played striker, until he scored.

In the third game of the season, disaster struck. I continued to struggle to get Eamon to stop dribbling so much, trying everything I could think of to get him to see the light. Eamon improved on this, but still wasn't playing the center mid position as unselfishly as I felt he should—pass first and shoot second, wanting whoever played this central position to make everyone around him better through his distribution, ala the conversations about Magic Johnson.

Instead, Eamon kept wanting to take a defender on with his dribbling skills and look for his own shot, before he looked to pass.

I kept trying to convince Eamon to change. "If you fake out a defender enough times with your moves, you're just putting a target on your back. Some day one of these defenders is going to get pissed off and take you down from behind. It's already happened a few times. You're a talented player, but you're playing with fire, setting yourself up to be hurt. If you're in the 18, then sure, go ahead and feel free to take a defender on and go to goal, but if you're in the mid-field away from goal, please move the ball quickly, play one- and two-touch soccer."

Eamon was the only player on the team who came close to rivaling Little Charlie and Musie's ball control, but he was also one of the most stubborn and hard-headed players I'd ever coached. Eamon was headed to play at Whitman College next year, a very competitive D3 college up in Walla, Washington. He had his soccer future all laid out.

In the third league game, on the Shoreline field, playing a team from Sultan, what I told Eamon might happen, happened. He put a move on a defender, and the defender sprinted after him after being juked and took Eamon down from behind. Eamon grabbed his knee, screaming in pain. He tore his ACL. His hopes of playing college soccer now shattered, at least for a year or two. Turned out Eamon never played college soccer. However, because of his experience in rehab after his surgery, he graduated with a degree in physical training and went on to become a physical therapist. Who knows? Maybe things do happen for a reason.

The fourth game of the season, without Eamon, but with Jake and Musie playing as our center mids, the team met up with a strong team from Stanwood. The Internationals ended up winning 4–1, but this one was more of a battle than the previous games had been. The season continued with the Internationals winning a few routs, as well as a few relatively close games, though none were a major challenge. The closest game so far was the one played in Stanwood, where we won by three goals.

Mid-season, I was contacted by Chris, who played goalie for a strong club team from the south end.

I knew his team and his coach from way back when we first played in the LPT Tournament, the first club team the Internationals played; the team that beat us in a PK shoot-out when Russ insisted on shuffling the PK lineup at the last minute. Their coach and I had also been in the same soccer licensing course several years back.

I was concerned about not having a backup goalie, so I invited Chris to the next practice. We let the guys take shots on him. He looked fairly decent, moving well laterally, but it was also clear he wouldn't be giving Emi a run for the money.

Still, the team needed a backup goalie in case Emi was sick or injured, so Chris was added to the roster. He lived in the Renton area, at least an hour's drive away.

I told Chris that he'd be the backup goalie and would likely only get in a game if the team was way up or way down or if Emi was hurt or couldn't make a game. I wanted Chris to know this upfront since he lived a long distance away. I also offered, because of the long drive, if he wanted, he only had to attend one practice a week.

Around this same time, another player was welcomed to our team. Gunnar Ildhuso III had played with Jake and Eamon at King's. Gunnar's family was from Norway, and his dad was one of the largest seafood distributors in the state. Gunnar, like Eamon, was an All-Conference player. He also happened to be left-footed, and it is advantageous to have a player who can cross the ball accurately or take shots from the left side of the field. Only about 18% of all soccer players are left-footed. Jake and Eamon told me about Gunnar before the season started, but Gunnar had been recovering from a concussion and was restricted from playing until this point in the season.

Gunnar Ildhuso III

The season continued, and the International team continued to run the table, winning every game. In a game, again versus Sultan, this time at the Sultan field, another of our players was injured. Sultan was the same team we played when Eamon tore his ACL. At this game, Ben suffered a severe high ankle sprain. An ankle sprain can sometimes take longer to heal than even a broken bone. Ben would be out for the rest of the season and probably for state cup play as well. He turned out to be a strong player, better than I'd anticipated, but the team still had enough talent on the bench to overcome his loss.

The Internationals were undefeated, but the last game of the regular season was coming up, and we'd be playing FC Edmonds Vipers, a very good team we'd played several competitive friendlies against in past seasons. Jake played on the Vipers a few years before, so he knew many of the players on the team.

Right before the game, Jake heard the Vipers were going to play five in their mid-field to try to shut down the International's passing lanes. A common belief in soccer is that games are won and lost in the mid-field. Jake and Randy suggested we do something to counteract this strategy. The coaches discussed this a bit and then decided to do the same, hoping this would throw the Vipers off their plan.

I'd soon regret this decision. The Internationals were the better team and should not have adjusted. We should've stuck to the game plan, which had been successful in countless games before and against better teams than the Vipers.

I also made another major bone-headed decision.

I wanted to give Chris, making the long drive from Renton to come to practices, more playing time, and so I let him play half the game and Emi the other half. I started Chris, figuring Emi would play the more critical half, the second period.

Emi wasn't happy about not starting, but I said it was only fair to give Chris some time in goal since he'd been making the long commute.

The Internationals had already clinched the League Championship, which was one of the reasons I started Chris, but still, we wanted to remain undefeated.

The center ref, Blake, was the same age as the players on the field. Blake knew many players on the International team as they were from the same high school and also because he played on the local rival rec team, The Stars, the local rivals back when we were the Mad Dogs. I later discovered that Blake was not scheduled to be the center ref for this game. He was slated to be the AR, the assistant ref, but he asked the AR to switch with him for this game. Blake had been named Young Ref for the State of Washington, as had his older brother before him. In fact, his older brother had asked me to write a reference letter for him when he applied to be voted Young Ref of the Year, and I wrote him a glowing endorsement. I also knew the AR, Steve, from officiating many of the Internationals games. Steve and I got along well and shared mutual respect for one another.

The game started, and it wasn't long before the Vipers scored a decent shot, but one that Emi would've likely stopped. Fifteen minutes later, they scored again. Emi would have definitely stopped this shot. The Internationals were out of whack. I soon changed back to our usual 4-4-2 formation and subbed Emi in for Chris at goalie. These adjustments instantly began to change the momentum of the game. The Internationals scored and were now one goal behind.

Play continued for another 15 minutes, when just before half-time, Gunnar was dribbling toward the goal. He was just outside the 18 box, not a single Viper defender, other than their Keeper, between him and the goal.

Gunnar had a powerful and accurate shot and looked like he was well on his way to scoring a goal, or at least a great opportunity for him to score, when a Viper player grabbed him from behind and pulled him back, holding onto both of Gunnar's shoulders—a foul in any league in the world that would often even result in a red card. The ref didn't blow the whistle or even card the offending player. Their defender had probably cost Gunnar and the International team a goal.

I yelled out to Blake, the young ref, "That was a goal scoring opportunity; that's an absolute card. Why didn't you call that?"

The ref shouted back, "That's enough, Coach," but I persisted. "How could you not see that?"

The ref yelled, "Not another word out of you."

When I insisted, "He totally grabbed our player by both shoulders," the young ref said, "One more word, and I'm going to card you. Randy then rushed over to calm me down."

Ten minutes later, right before the first half ended, Pemba was fouled and went down to the ground holding his arm in pain. He lay near the center circle for a few minutes. I asked the AR, Steve, if I could go on the field and check up on Pemba. Steve waved me on. I ran over to Pemba and talked to him. He was hurt and had to come out of the game. I wasn't sure how bad Pemba's injury was, but knew he was extremely tough and shared his father's Sherpa grit. I'd never seen Pemba injured before, so if he was in pain, it was probably bad. I was considering if Pemba should be taken to the ER.

After checking on Pemba, I turned to Blake, the ref, and calmly asked, "Why didn't you card that player? You had to see it."

Blake replied, "That's it! I warned you," and showed me a red card.

I was stunned. "A red card? Are you kidding? For what?"

"I told you to be quiet, and I also didn't wave you on the field. You're not allowed to come onto the field without my permission."

"I asked the AR's permission, and he waved me on...go ask him."

Blake shook his head and huffed. "Leave the field now."

Randy would now have to coach the team. In the 25 years I'd coached youth soccer, I was never carded, not even a yellow card, and now I had been given a red card. This meant I would miss the rest of this game and wouldn't be able to coach in the first game of the state cup...this, in my last season coaching the Internationals. I spoke to Randy briefly, and then drove Pemba home so his mother, Fur, could take her son to the hospital. I asked her to let me know how I could help, and told her I'd check on Pemba later that evening to see how he was doing.

I then called Randy to get the update. Randy said that not long after I was carded, Jake, his son, was red carded as well. Another first. Never had one of my players been red carded before, and given I'd coached players with hair-trigger tempers like Essa, Gerardo, and even Little Charlie, this was either a great accomplishment or a minor miracle. Before games, I'd be sure to tell Gerardo to keep cool and relay this on to Little Charlie as well. I used to worry about Essa in this regard as well, but over the years, he'd done an increasingly great job of learning to control his temper.

I explained to our players prone to outbursts, that soccer is a great place to learn how to control one's temper, that when people get so mad and see red, they can't see clearly—a time when they can make life-changing mistakes. I told my players about a time early on in my coaching career. The boys were only about six to seven years old at the time and the coaches at that age group and younger were required to ref their own games. We were playing a game where, a boy on the other team, who was about a head taller than all the others, kept throwing his elbows out and hitting our players in the head. He was not only athletic, but uber-aggressive too. Because I was the ref that game, I would tell the boy that he wasn't allowed to throw his elbows out. However, the young boy persisted in doing this and putting the opposing players in harm's way. After warning him a number of times, I began awarding the ball to my team whenever he would throw his elbow out.

Soon, I start hearing a parent shouting from the sidelines, in a loud voice, "Let them play, it's a man's game, let them play". I tried to ignore this, but the man kept shouting louder and louder. He seemed to have some type of accent, maybe European? I wasn't sure, but I was sure he was getting on my nerves. I tried to explain to the man that I was just trying to keep the boys safe, but he persisted in yelling, and doing so, progressively louder.

"You Americans don't know this game. Let them play!" he shouted.

This tirade went on for at least a half hour or more. I was becoming more and more frustrated. Finally, the game ended, and I quickly grabbed my son and headed to our car, parked on the street nearby. After being yelled at by this obnoxious parent for such a long time, I was now livid. However, these were six and seven-year-old boys. What could I do?

We got to the car, and suddenly I see this loud and insulting parent running towards me. He didn't look much bigger than me; though wiry and athletic looking.

At this point, there *were* no other boys or parents around, so I thought to myself, okay, game on. I put my son in the car and stood ready to face this guy. He approaches, and I'm ready to rumble. He gets close and says in his accent, "I'm really sorry, man. I just lost it. I know you were just trying to keep the boys safe. I'm so sorry," as he extended his hand.

I quickly calmed down, relieved, I shook his hand and we talked for a while. I found out he just moved here from Canada, where his son played a lot of hockey, which was why he was throwing his elbows out so often. The guy proceeded to tell me he'd been the French National Kick-boxing Champion, and that he was opening a training studio in the area. This man would have made mince-meat out of me. I'd have had all my teeth kicked in!

So, as I told my players, the moral of the story is: you never know who you're getting into it with. Maybe the other person has a black belt in Karate, or maybe he's packing a gun or carrying a big knife. You just don't know. So be smart and do your best to keep your cool.

"If you get a red card, you're not only suspended for the remainder of the game and the next game, but you've put your team in jeopardy having to play a man down. You can cost your team the game. However, on the streets, losing your temper can cost you your life or the life of whoever's with you. If you learn to control your temper in the game, you'll probably learn to control it when you face other tough situations in your life."

We tied the score, and the game ended in a 2–2 draw. This didn't hurt the Internationals, other than the loss of pride drawing with a lesser team. The Internationals had already clinched the league title.

I had to request a meeting with the WSYA Disciplinary Committee to try to get mine and Jake's red card rescinded. I got in touch with Steve, the AR, who confirmed he'd given me permission to go on the field, and that he had shared that info with Blake after the game. He added that he was supposed to be the center ref for that game, but that Blake had asked to switch with him. Now Steve was curious as to why Blake asked him to switch responsibilities. He also shared that Blake had accused me of screaming in his face and using profanity.

"That never happened," I said. "Not even close."

"I know," Steve said. "I'll testify to that as well."

I met with the committee, knowing that the vast majority of the time, red cards were not rescinded.

This was an even more unusual situation, as it was the word of a ref voted Washington State Young Ref of the Year going up against the word of a coach who'd been voted Washington State Coach of the Year, surely the first time a situation like this had ever come up.

Steve was interviewed by the committee officials and told them in no uncertain terms that he waved me onto the field and also that he had made that clear to Blake after the game ended. He also told the committee officials that he was close enough to see and hear that I didn't raise my voice or use foul language directed to the center ref or otherwise. He said that Blake was supposed to be the AR that game but had asked Steve to switch with him.

Normally, at least in Washington State, for youth soccer games the ref is at least two years older than the players they are officiating, at minimum.

The committee could see that Blake had clearly been lying and, after doing so, attempted to cover up his lies. Just about everything he'd accused me of was a complete misrepresentation of the truth.

The red card was thankfully rescinded, and I was eligible to continue coaching the team in state cup. Jake's red card, however, was not rescinded, and he'd miss the first game of the state tournament. I'd never forgive Blake. I later ran into Blake's parents at some mutual friends' parties, but we never spoke about what happened. As far as I was concerned, Blake was persona non grata from that point on.

I held no grudge against the Vipers.

What happened with the ref wasn't their fault, so when the Vipers' coach offered we play a friendly to prepare for the upcoming state cup, I agreed to do so, with the provision that both coaches make sure the game was kept safe in order to minimize the risk of any player on either team being injured before state cup play began. The team then took a few weeks off to rest, recuperate, and enjoy the holidays.

CHAPTER 15

THE FINAL CHAPTER

In the week after Christmas and before New Year's, I got an extremely upsetting call from Jennifer, the doctor who'd sponsored Little Charlie. Jennifer, in a shaky voice, shared that Charlie had been despondent after the end of the soccer season and had attempted to take his life. Apparently, Charlie had been in contact with his friends back home and had found out that one of his closest friends had been shot and killed in a gang-related shooting. This was apparently too much for Charlie to bear. Why was he in such a nice place, when his friends weren't? Why did he deserve to be alive?

This all took place during the holidays, away from his friends and everything familiar to him. This was also a time when the team had shut down for the holidays and there were no practices or games to go to. Charlie was depressed, angry, sad, confused; and in a moment of impulse, he attempted to take his life by strangling himself. This was obviously a cry for help. An attempt, in his mind, to possibly atone for all his wrong-doings. A way to stop the pain and confusion he felt about all the "bad things" he'd done earlier in his life. He had hurt others, and now he would hurt himself.

Fortunately, Jennifer found him in time. He was rushed to the hospital where he stayed a few days to make sure he was okay. However, because of this attempt on his life, she knew he had to go back to Guatemala where he could work out things in his native land, where he could effectively communicate. Jennifer helped him find counseling in Guatemala.

She went on to say the only time Charlie appeared truly happy was when he knew he had a practice or a game with his team coming up.

This was sad and shocking news for all of the players on our team. Charlie was an especially gifted soccer player, and all the guys loved him. He had an infectious smile and incredible enthusiasm and charisma. He literally lit up with love for the game and for his teammates, embracing all of us in his unbridled jubilation. In retrospect, Charlie's highs were so high, that maybe this was a sign of his condition. Though he spoke little English, he did fluently speak the universal language of genuine love for the game, the common bond for all the players on FC Shoreline International. Little Charlie would be sorely missed by all of us.

Fortunately, we later found out that Charlie, with his now more polished skills and the understanding that there were people who truly cared about him and with Jennifer and Sean continuing to visit Charlie and help him both emotionally and financially, his condition improved and he later went on to play professional soccer in the First Division, the highest level in Guatemala. Thank God there are people in this world like Jennifer, a true angel on Charlie's shoulder, devoted to always watching out for him.

* * *

It was early January 2010, and the team was preparing for the state cup tournament, our final weeks as a team. Randy secured the beautiful turf field at King's High School on a Saturday for a friendly vs. the Edmonds Vipers. Chris, the backup goalie, had quit the team after he was pulled that last regular season when he allowed in two very saveable goals. That was history now, but it did leave the Internationals without a backup goalie.

I had several players on the team who, with very little goalie training, could do at least a decent job in securing the net. I always told my players that if we played defense as we should, our keeper shouldn't even touch the ball. It took 10 other players to allow a shot on goal. I knew this was a bit of an exaggeration, but there was a good deal of truth to this, as well.

The game was on, and both teams struggled to score when, early in the second half, Riyen, our speedy right mid from Holland, got behind the Vipers' defense and scored. About 15 minutes later, a long ball headed toward the International goal with a Viper attacker chasing after it. Emi went to ground to stop the ball. He laid his body out to protect himself as every goalie is trained to do and extended his hands to grab the incoming ball. As he extended, the incoming attacker stepped on his hand. Emi yelled out in pain. The ball was knocked away, but Emi was injured. There were about 15 minutes left in the game. Not having anyone to back up Emi in goal, I had the game called. I was upset, as was our team, but we also were aware it wasn't intentional. The attacker should've stopped, though, the game being a friendly, but he'd tried to score and one couldn't completely blame him. I nevertheless had had enough of this ill-fated Viper team to last a lifetime.

I found a hand specialist for Emi and made an appointment for him to be checked out and X-rayed. As suspected, his thumb was broken. For any other player on the field, a broken thumb wouldn't hinder him from playing, but for a goalie, playing with a broken thumb was impossible. Emi was now lost for the state tournament.

Arguably the best goalie the team ever had could now no longer play for the team in its most important tournament. I took Emi to several doctor appointments and covered all the bills, as he and his family had no medical insurance.

The state cup was a few weeks away when, being the resourceful and admittedly obsessive personality, I am, I immediately began the search for a goalie. My first call was to Ethan, now attending Western

Washington University up in Bellingham. No dice. Ethan might be able to make a game or two, but he couldn't commit to making all of the games, though he wished he could.

Next call was to Dorian, the goalie for the Jetstream a few years back. He had also been the keeper for Shorewood High School, as well as the running back and linebacker on the high school football team. Dorian was six feet tall, built like a tank, and was a superb athlete. It was debatable who was the better keeper, Emi or Dorian? What wasn't debatable was that both Emi and Dorian were incredible goalkeepers that any team would be thrilled to have. Dorian was indeed available as well as excited to play. He had just played for the Edmonds CC team, just as Tim had, but he'd be available for State Cup play.

Finding a goalie as talented as Dorian was like a gift from above.

Dorian Lair

*   *   *

The International's first game was against SC United Fire, a fairly strong team from the Stanwood area, one we'd already played and beat in league.

Musie scored the first goal on a well-placed cross delivered from Gunnar. The next goal was scored by Gerardo after a cross from Essa. The third goal also came from a cross from Essa, this time Tim was the beneficiary.

Tim had re-joined the team shortly after his season at Edmonds Community College had ended. The Fire scored next on a corner kick, when their player who received the kick passed to one of his teammates who was unmarked inside the 18 and scored on a low shot that found the inside far corner. With 20 minutes left in the game, Tim scored again on another assist from Essa. The Internationals won 4–1. Essa finished with an assist hat-trick, an unofficial term but a worthy accomplishment, nonetheless.

For the next state cup game, it looked like the Internationals might be in for a tough game. It was an away game, a three-hour drive to Aberdeen in the Grays Harbor area. At least 40 people were going to the game. I chartered a luxury bus and, like on other long trips, brought along soccer DVDs and comedy movies for all to watch. Sherri and other parents made sandwiches and treats, and we were on our way. The beef jerky made by Dorian's grandfather was delectable.

The team we were playing, the Pumas, had won the state championship in the recreational division. They played in this division because the players, mostly Hispanic, couldn't afford the several thousand dollars it cost to play club; but for all intents and purposes, they were a club team. The field in Aberdeen was a grass field, not in great shape but playable.

The Grays Harbor team offered the Internationals a strong challenge, but the FCS Internationals scored first when Jake headed in a beautifully placed corner kick sent from Gunnar. Gerardo scored next on an assist from Essa.

The final goal, in the second half, came from Peter, who'd moved up from his center back position on a corner kick, then scored after a great assist from Shivy. The Internationals won 3–0 and hadn't been tested as we'd expected we might be.

The team's third state cup game was against a fairly weak team from Ballard. The Internationals dominated the game and won 8–1. Musie started off the scoring, dribbling in the 18 unassisted, juking one defender after another before scoring with a well-placed shot. Musie's ball control early in the game sent the Ballard team a quick message they stood no chance in this game.

Gunnar and Musie each had hat-tricks, while Essa and Gerardo scored goals as well, with assists provided by Essa, Tim, Riyen. Musie and Jake. Our FC Shoreline International team had made it to the state championship game to be played at the Starfire soccer complex where we had won our first State Championship. We would be meeting the same Gray Harbor Puma team we had beaten in league and in the second game of the tournament.

Game day arrived, Saturday, February 27th, 2010. It was one of those typical Northwest winter days, overcast and drizzle. As was usual for our away games, we all met up at the Shorewood High School parking lot and caravanned to the game. Arriving there, we soon discovered that the game wasn't being played in the spacious and larger Starfire Stadium field, as one would have thought, given these were the oldest age teams in the state cup tournament. Instead the game was being played on a smaller field near the entrance to Starfire, below and adjacent to the Mad Dog Pizza restaurant. Maybe the fact that we were near Mad Dog Pizza was a good omen?"

Randy, myself, and many of our players recognized several of the refs for this game. The center ref was a fairly heavy-set guy, a lazy sort of Ref, the kind who didn't like to move too much. He would barely jog up and down the field, clearly compromised in his desire and possibly even his ability to keep up with the speed of a game at this level. One of the assistant refs was a bespectacled tall, thin, older man who the boys remembered from a past game, when he'd allowed a goal on a shot that hit the side netting. None of us recognized the other assistant ref. We knew at least two of the refs weren't the caliber one would expect to be officiating a state championship game.

A sizable crowd came to the game—parents, family, friends, and fans for both teams. Ethan, our team's former goalie, even journeyed down from Bellingham to play in the game to serve as a backup to Dorian. Emi and Ben were also there to root for their team, though both were still injured and unable to play.

The game began, and within just a few minutes, Essa scored on an assist from Gerardo. I thought the game might turn into a rout...at least I hoped. We hadn't had much trouble beating this team just a few weeks earlier and doing so on their home field. Gunnar scored the second goal not long after, when he took a hard shot that rebounded off their goalie, which he then knocked into the goal. The Internationals scored again when Essa got behind their defense and fired a rocket into the upper V. The AR with the thick glasses, however, raised his flag and called off-sides. The coaches and International bench were close to the play and knew Essa hadn't been off-sides, but the heavy-set, slow-footed center ref was too far from the action to overrule the vision-impaired AR. The goal was annulled.

The Pumas scored right before halftime when their best attacker, playing on the left flank, eluded Tim and then juked Milen and fired off a hard, unsaveable ground shot into the corner of the net. The half ended with the Internationals up 2 - 1.

After the game resumed, it wasn't long before Gerardo scored on an assist from Musie. The ref again called off-sides, though this time it was the Center Ref and not the "visually impaired" AR wearing the thick glasses. This call was also not as clear-cut as the last call had been. Off-sides calls are among the difficult to make in soccer, and refs often get it wrong. Goal-line technology and video review weren't available as they are today, not that they would've been available anyway in a youth soccer tournament.

Then calamity struck. One of their attackers had the ball at the intersection of the outside corner of the 18 area and the goal-line. He had his back to Musie who was defending him when he flopped to the ground. The center ref was far from the play as was the AR, and the attacker had his back to both referees, so they didn't have a clear view of the play when the center ref called a foul and awarded the Pumas a PK.

We could all clearly see that their player had intentionally flopped, but nothing could be done once the ref made the call. It was also not a goal scoring opportunity. No ref worth his salt would normally make a questionable game-changing call like this in a championship game and especially in the corner of the 18 and the goal-line where there was no opportunity whatsoever for the attacking player to score a goal. Overlooking the exact spot where the foul supposedly occurred was the balcony of the Mad Dog Pizza restaurant with a number of fans up above watching the game. Folks sitting up there had a birds-eye view of the play and later informed us there was definitely no foul on that play. Nevertheless, fans and observers don't make the calls, refs do, and the call had been made.

I had instructed Dorian earlier that if there was a PK, "Don't try to guess which side you think the shot will go and try to dive wide right or left. Just hold the middle and try to save whatever you can save a few feet in either direction. If the shooter is skilled enough to hit the inside corners, then so be it." I felt many goal keepers tried to guess and would too often overcommit to one side or another, and then the kick would often go straight up the middle, where the keeper had just been standing.

As stated, Dorian was an extremely talented goalie, but I'd seen him try to guess the direction a kick was going back when he played for Shorewood High School. Coaches often differ on this advice. Some, in fact, maybe even most coaches and keeper trainers want their goalie to rely on their instinct and go for it.

At the professional and college levels, the keeper is trained to watch the PK kickers' eyes, feet, and body language, then react accordingly. A sort of educated guess. However, even at the very highest levels of play, I'd seen goalkeepers often guess incorrectly and end up going the wrong way. At the high school and similar age levels, I knew kickers weren't usually that accurate or consistent with their placement to justify this approach; which was why I always counseled my goalkeepers to just do their best to hold the middle and try to save whatever they could to either side.

Habits being what they are, combined with the fact this was the first PK Dorian would face while playing for the Internationals, Dorian guessed wrong and dove to his left...the PK instead went up the center. The score was tied. If our guys didn't now have a serious case of the heebie-jeebies, I know I sure did.

The Internationals still controlled the game, but we couldn't seem to score even though we had numerous opportunities. We had at least fifteen or twenty shots while our opponent only had a few, none being very dangerous, other than their one earlier goal. Most of our shots went over, went wide or were hit straight to the Keeper; their Keeper also made a few nice saves. Plus, we had the three goals called back on questionable off-sides calls. It was just one of those kinds of games and as every coach knows, anything can happen when you don't put the ball in the back of the net. If you've played or coached the game for any decent amount of time; you've had those games where your team totally dominated, maybe even out-shot the other team twenty or more to one and you lost the game. This one was looking like it could be one of those nightmare kind of games. The clock was winding down, the game seemingly headed for overtime when, with less than a minute left in regulation time, Essa got the ball near the 30-yard line and saw Jake making a run from his defensive center mid position. Essa sent a long pass up to Jake. The Puma goalie came out of the box to try to win the ball, he got a hand on it, but couldn't control it and Jake ran in before the keeper could recover and tapped the ball into the open goal. Hallelujah!

A minute or so later—though to all the International players, coaches and fans, it seemed like an eternity—the ref blew the final whistle to signal the end of the game.

The International players and coaches all ran onto the field, hugging Jake, Essa, and whomever they could get to in a mad, chaotic celebration.

The Internationals had won the Washington State Championship once again. The second time in three years. When the celebration calmed down, we shook hands with the Pumas who'd put up a good battle. At the ceremony immediately following the game's end, the players and coaches each received bright yellow scarves from the Tournament Director that read: "Washington Youth Soccer Tournament Cup Champions—2010."

During the ceremony, Gerardo told me he was thinking about Little Charlie and that he was going to send him his scarf. That got me tearing up, which, being the emotional type, admittedly didn't take much. I told Gerardo how thoughtful his gesture was, but then asked that he keep his scarf. I told him I'd go to the tournament office and get Charlie one of his own.

As I walked to the office, I couldn't help but feel a bit down. We'd just won the state championship in our final season together. Why was I feeling this way? I thought back to the first year when we started out on this journey, the Thunder-Foot/Mad Dogs team I'd taken over so many years ago... how that team was transformed into the team it was today, FC Shoreline International.

I recalled how we had become an extended family and the many great times, the awesome international feasts, the lifelong memories we'd all shared. It wasn't all about the winning, never was...though, naturally it mattered.

It was about all of the wonderful people who had become such an important part of each other's lives, people from so many diverse backgrounds, nationalities, races, religions, and beliefs, never judging one another, never caring about who believed what or who had money or who didn't or any other superficial silliness...we just loved one another and enjoyed so many incredible experiences together. Being part of the International team had enriched every player and family, but none more so than me.

After this final International feast and team party we'd soon celebrate, I realized I might never see many of them again, a sad thought that washed over my heart when I went to pick up Little Charlie's championship scarf.

THE END

Celebration photo taken after the championship game

AUTHOR'S NOTES

When coaching our International team, it was clear that our team was unique. While at away games, I'd often notice people studying our team, trying to figure out how our mélange of players of many different races and cultures came to be. Some would even occasionally approach one of the parents, players or coaches and ask where we were from and how it happened that we had players from so many races and nationalities. Our team name, "International" also provoked people's curiosity.

We had so many incredible experiences during our years together that I always felt that many readers might find our team's story interesting. The catalyst for writing this book came after hearing our President speak disparagingly about immigrants, referring to them as criminals, drug dealers and rapists, as animals, not even people. That vilification of immigrants was especially hurtful to me, as I'd grown so close to our players and their families. I felt like someone was denigrating my own family, I took this personally.

It's never made sense to me why some people hate others for the color of their skin, religious beliefs or nationality. Our team proved we can be different and yet enjoy one another, learn from one another and embrace our differences rather than reject or castigate one another. How boring this world would be if we all looked the same, thought the same...

Regardless of what we look like or believe, we all want the same necessities for ourselves and our family—peace, good health, a safe haven with a roof over our heads, a comfortable bed to sleep in, clean water, enough food...

Instead, humanity has endured needless wars, hatred, bloodshed, racism and prejudice throughout history. My major at Cal Poly University was American history, where I made honor society, Phi Alpha Theta and understood that though our constitution advocates that "all men are created equal"; racism, prejudice and ostracism have nonetheless plagued our nation since its inception. Our country was founded by immigrants from many different countries. We're all the sons and daughters of immigrants.

While I understand that we can't have open borders and allow unfettered immigration, and that we need to carefully limit and vet immigrants who enter the US, I'll nevertheless always believe that all people should be treated with empathy and respect.

I'd like to thank Ilan Herman who helped mentor me through writing this book and provided expert oversight, editing and encouragement. I would also like to thank the kind folks at BookBaby for all of their help and support throughout the publishing process.

This story is entirely true! Nothing was added or embellished, other than having changed a few names, so as not to embarrass or demean anyone or in order to respect certain individuals' privacy. Naturally, this story wouldn't even exist were it not for the all of the players and their families. For every player that played on FC Shoreline International and every family that supported our team through the many years we were together, you will always be in my heart. I love you all and can never thank you enough for enriching my life as you have.

Thank you, readers, for taking time to read our story. I hope it touched you and left you believing that we can all live together in peace, love and harmony.

With love in my heart and hope for a better world,
Emerson Robbins

ABOUT THE AUTHOR

Emerson "Skip" Robbins, coached youth soccer for over 35 years, named Coach of the Year for Seattle in 2007, Coach of the Year for the State of Washington in 2008, COY for the Western U.S. in 2008, runner-up for National Coach of the Year in 2009.

His FC Shoreline International teams won two State Championships. Emerson graduated from Cal Poly University with honors in American History and went on to co-found national chain, Robbins Bros, Worlds Biggest Engagement Ring Stores and later founded, in the northwest EE Robbins, The Engagement Ring Store and Emerald City Marketing.

After coaching the FC Shoreline International team and retiring from business, Skip and the love of his life, wife, Sherri moved to the beach on Whidbey Island where he coached the local high school team for many years. Skip currently stays busy fishing, crabbing, playing pickleball as well as enjoying time with his family, four children and five grandchildren and continues to root for his home-town Seattle Seahawks and Sounders.